The Big Book of
Mandalas & Patterns
Coloring Pages

Variety Collection 1

By Genevieve Kiger Purdy

The Big Book of Mandalas & Patterns Coloring Pages
Variety Collection 1

This Book Belongs To

_____

The Big Book of Mandalas & Patterns Coloring Pages
Variety Collection 1

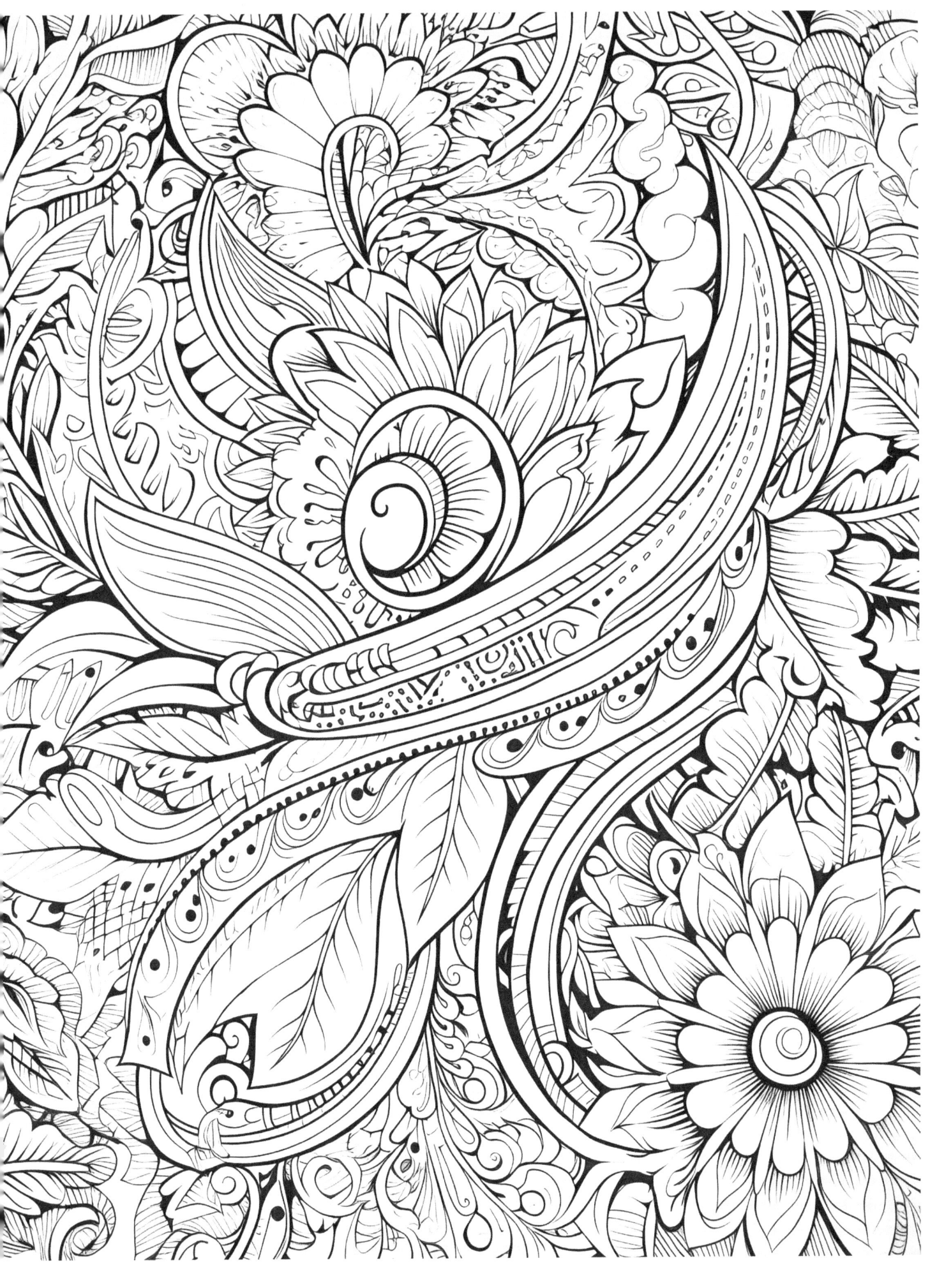

The Big Book of Mandalas & Patterns Coloring Pages
Variety Collection 1

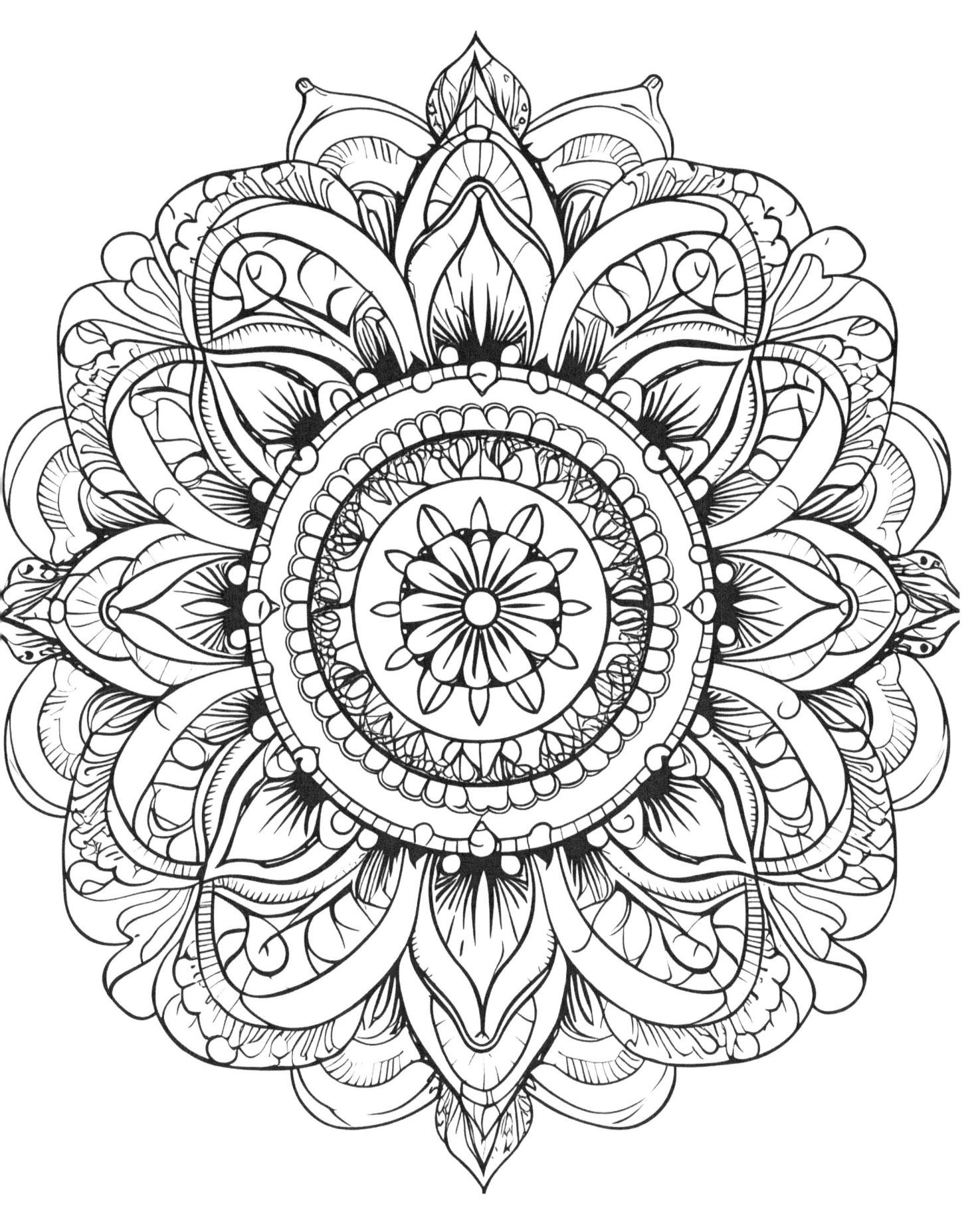

The Big Book of Mandalas & Patterns Coloring Pages
Variety Collection 1

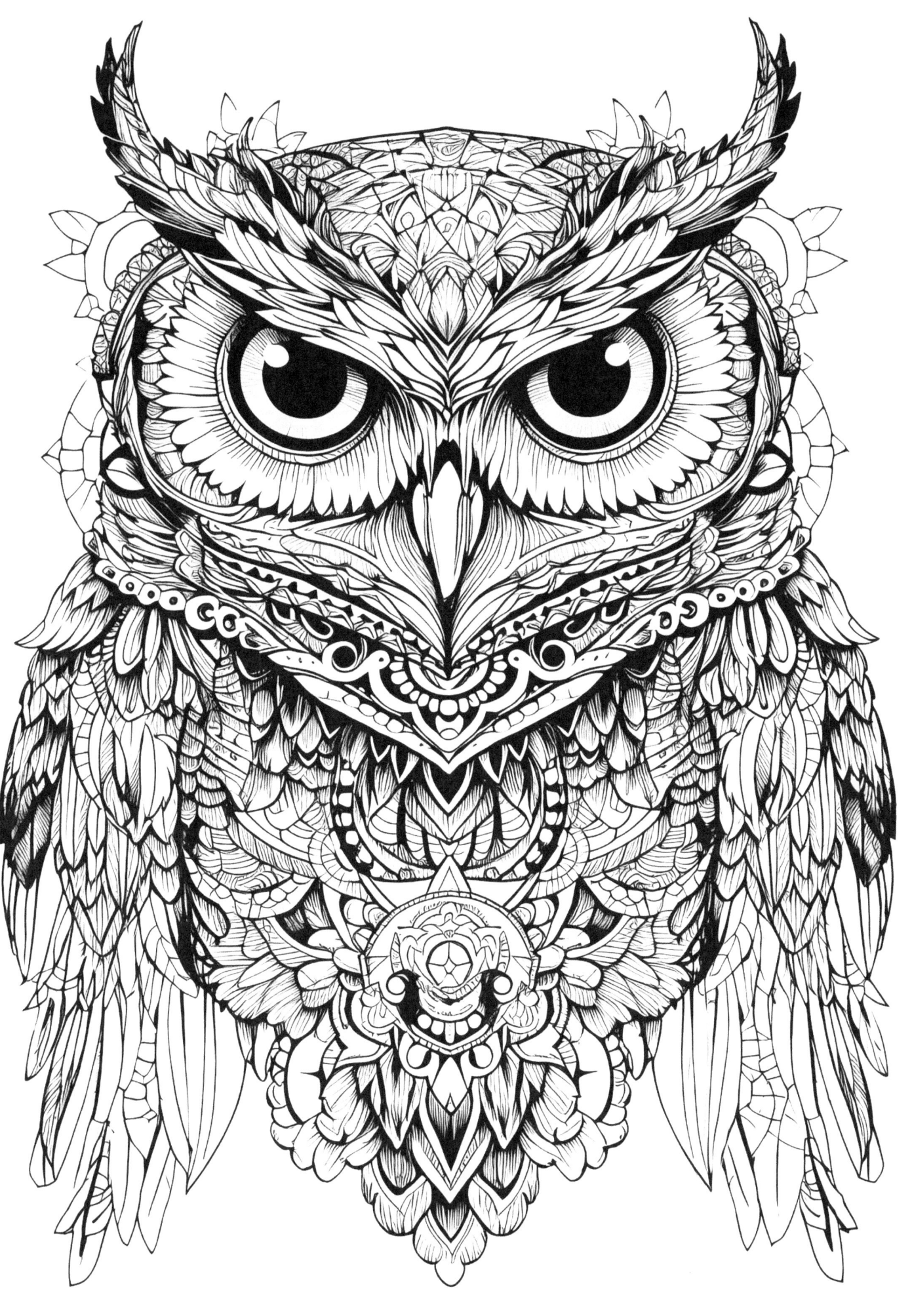

The Big Book of Mandalas & Patterns Coloring Pages
Variety Collection 1

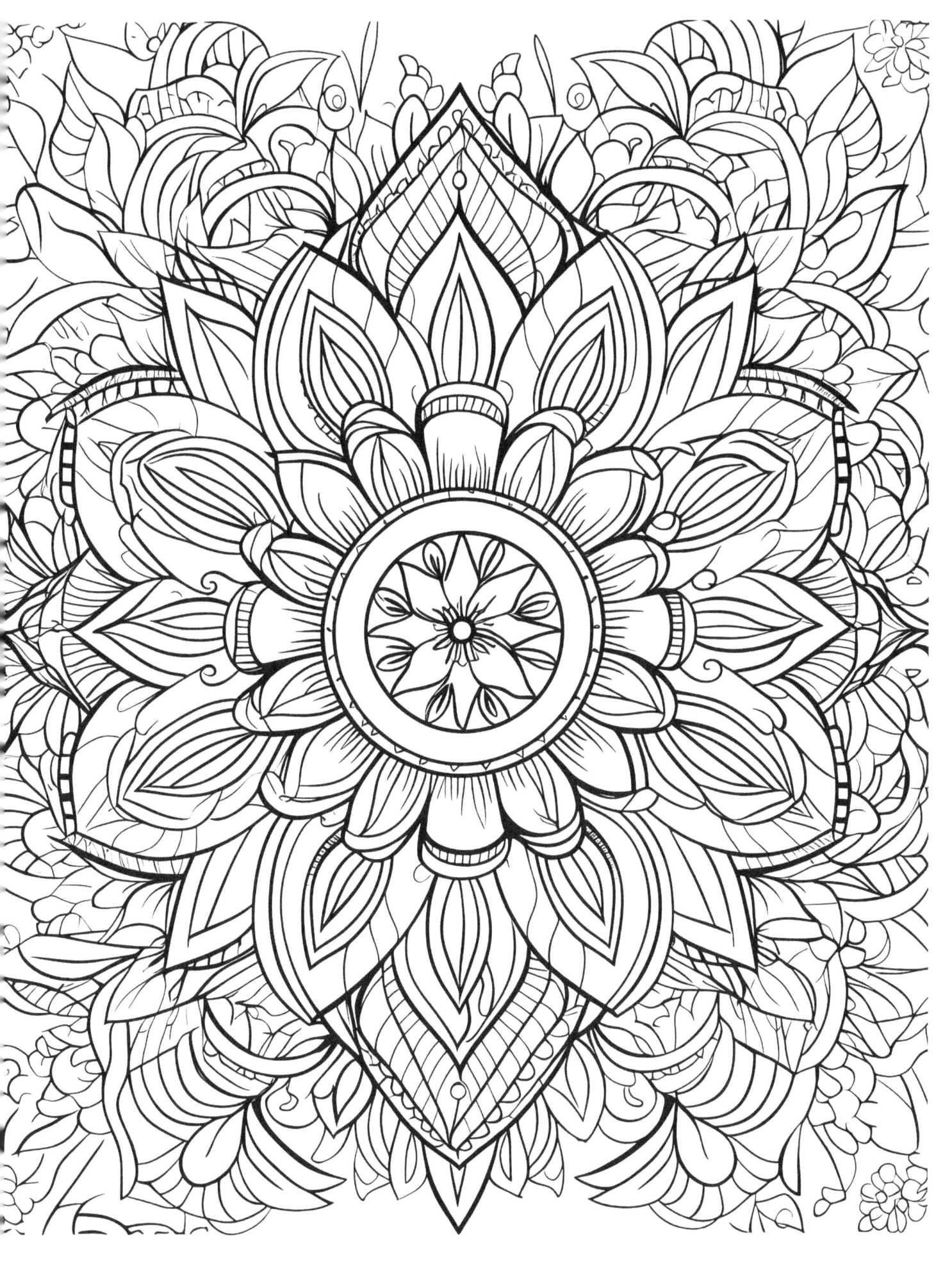

The Big Book of Mandalas & Patterns Coloring Pages
Variety Collection 1

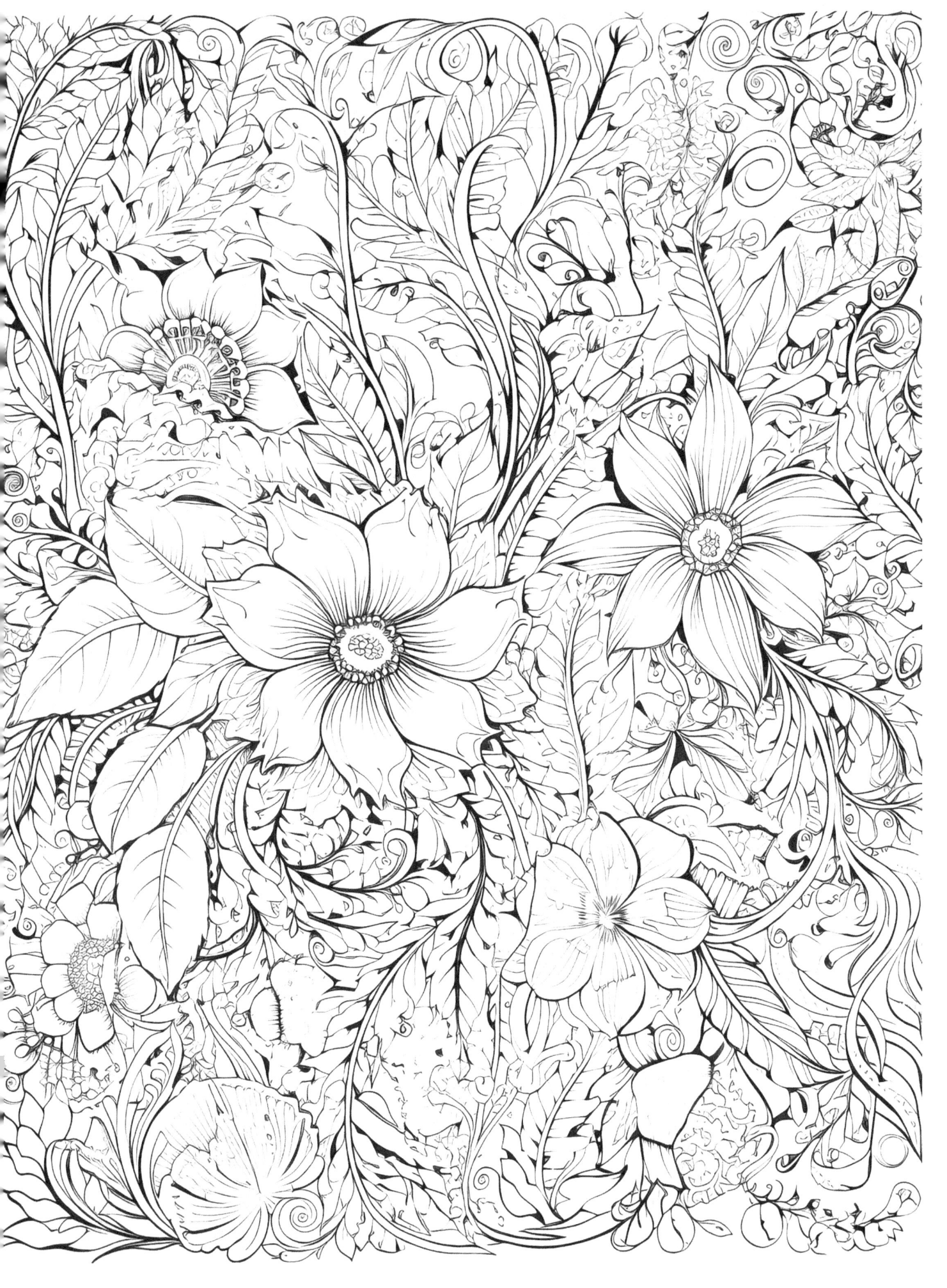

The Big Book of Mandalas & Patterns Coloring Pages
Variety Collection 1

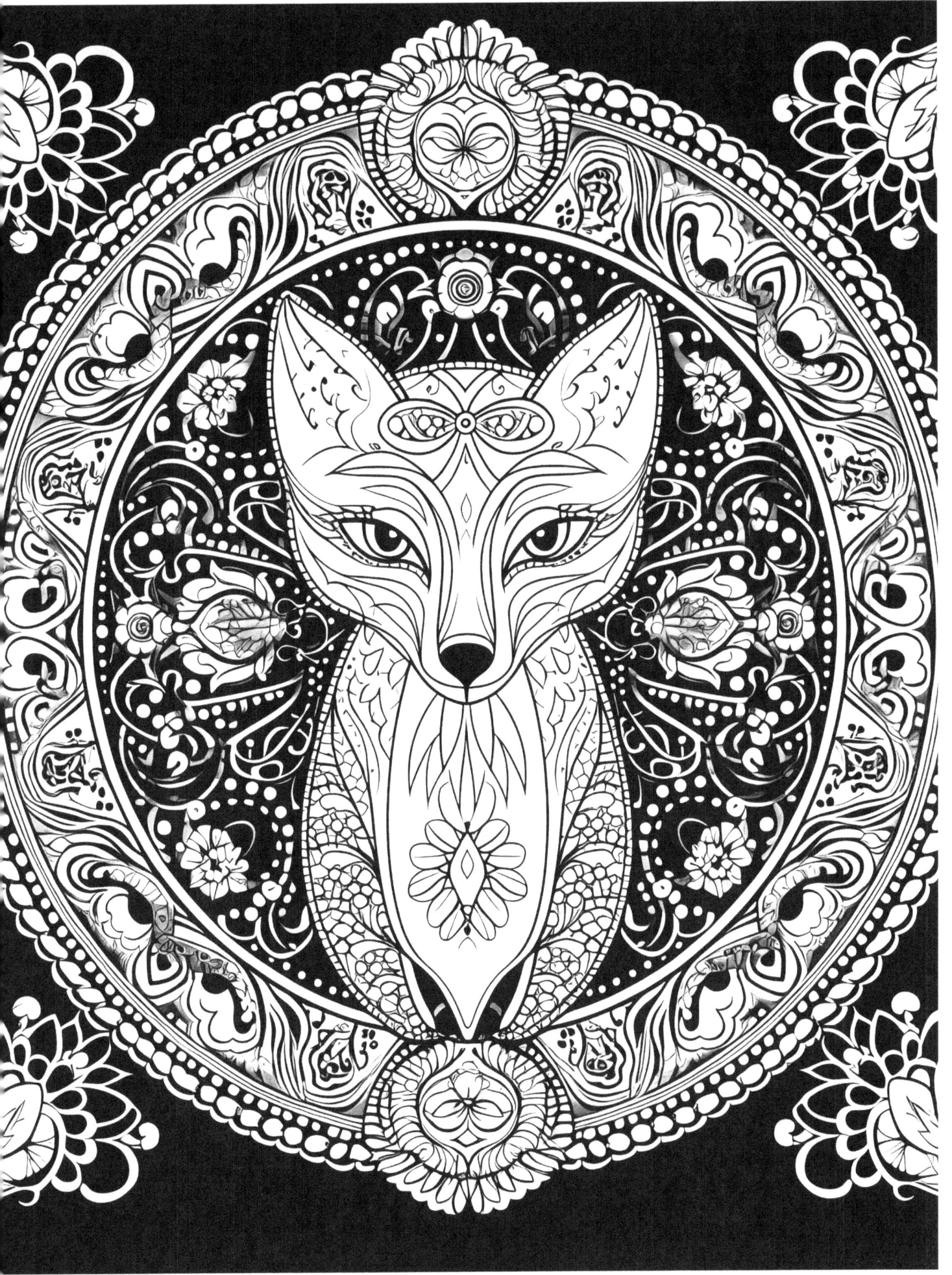

The Big Book of Mandalas & Patterns Coloring Pages
Variety Collection 1

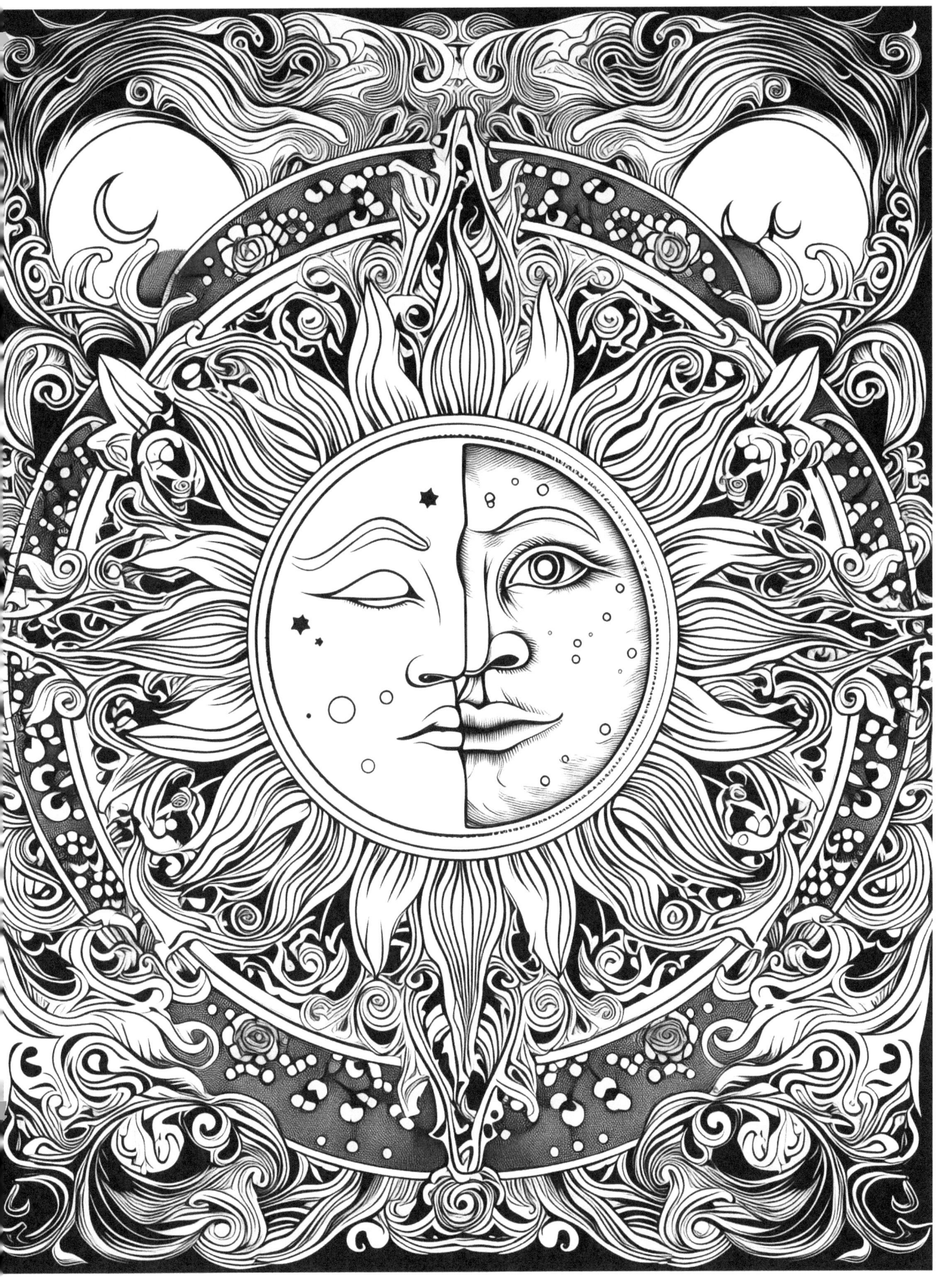

The Big Book of Mandalas & Patterns Coloring Pages
Variety Collection 1

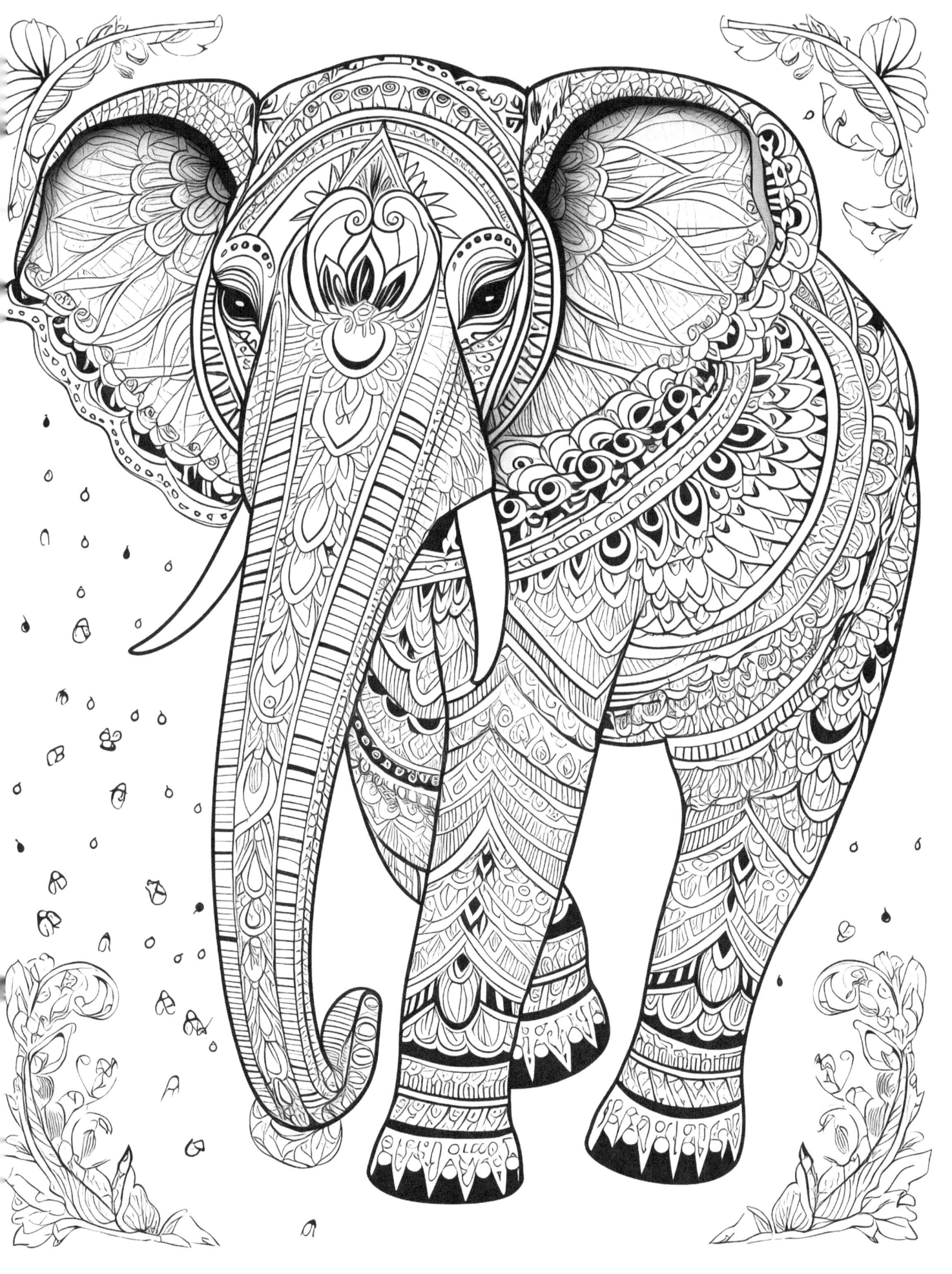

The Big Book of Mandalas & Patterns Coloring Pages
Variety Collection 1

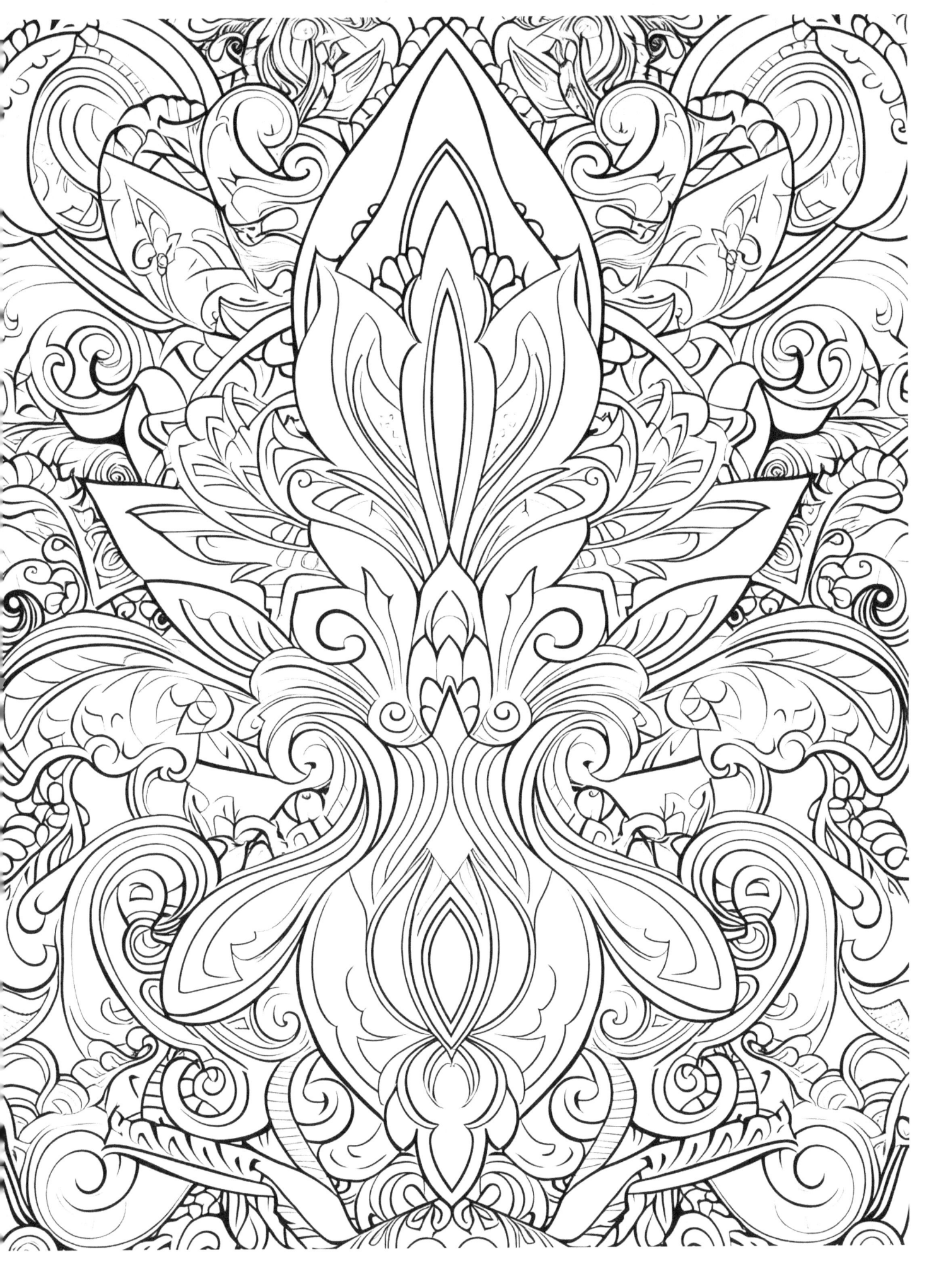

The Big Book of Mandalas & Patterns Coloring Pages
Variety Collection 1

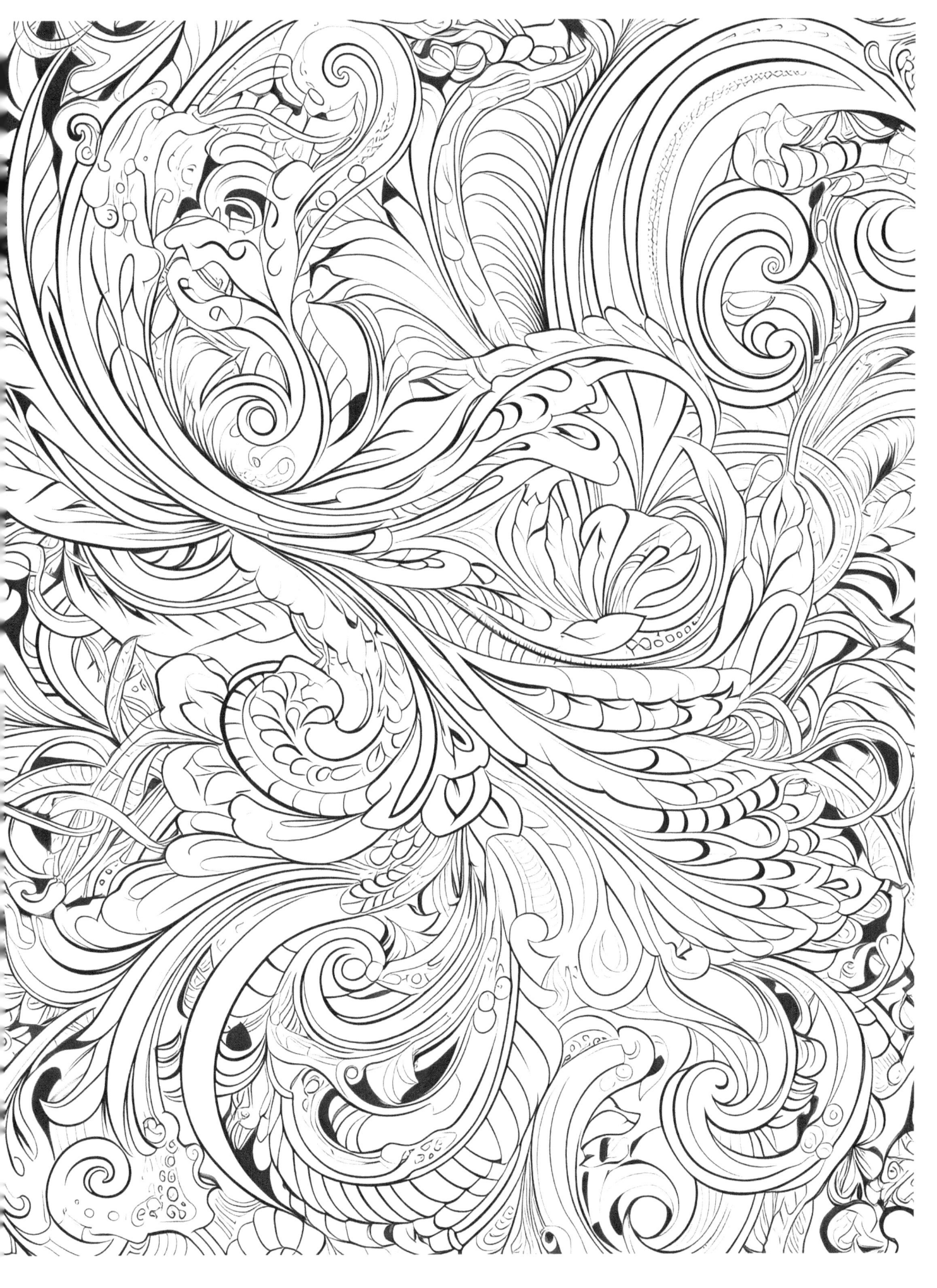

The Big Book of Mandalas & Patterns Coloring Pages
Variety Collection 1

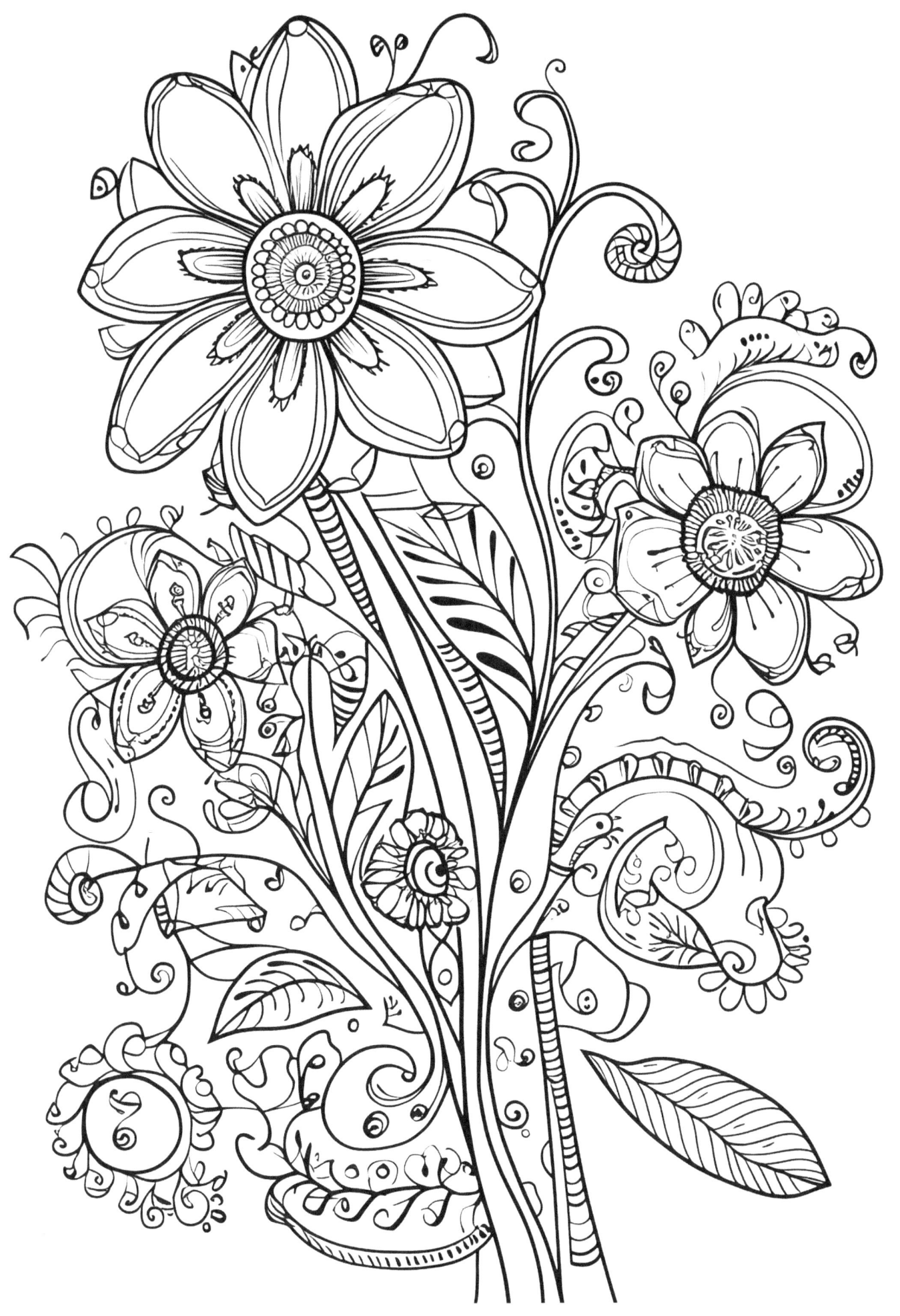

The Big Book of Mandalas & Patterns Coloring Pages
Variety Collection 1

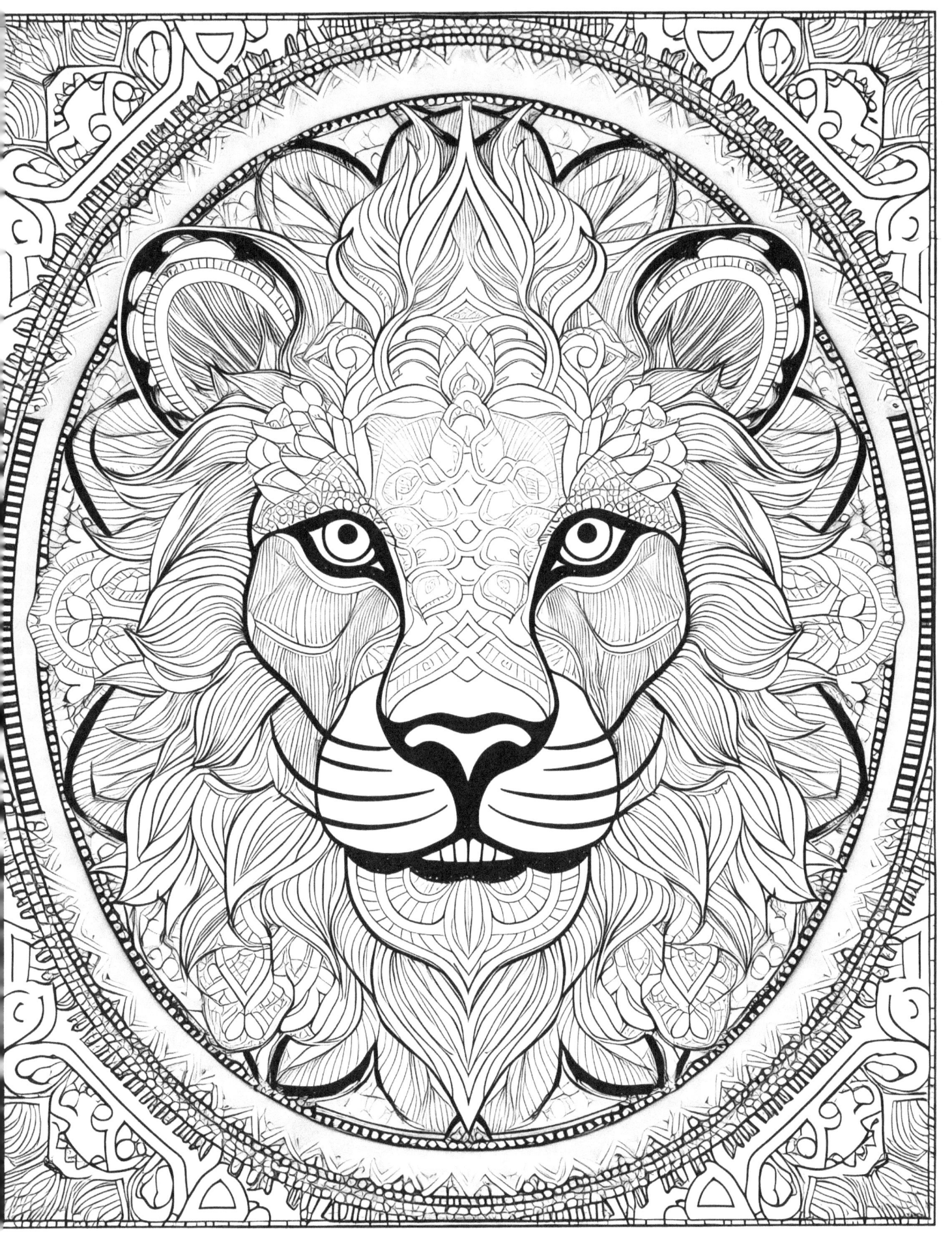

The Big Book of Mandalas & Patterns Coloring Pages
Variety Collection 1

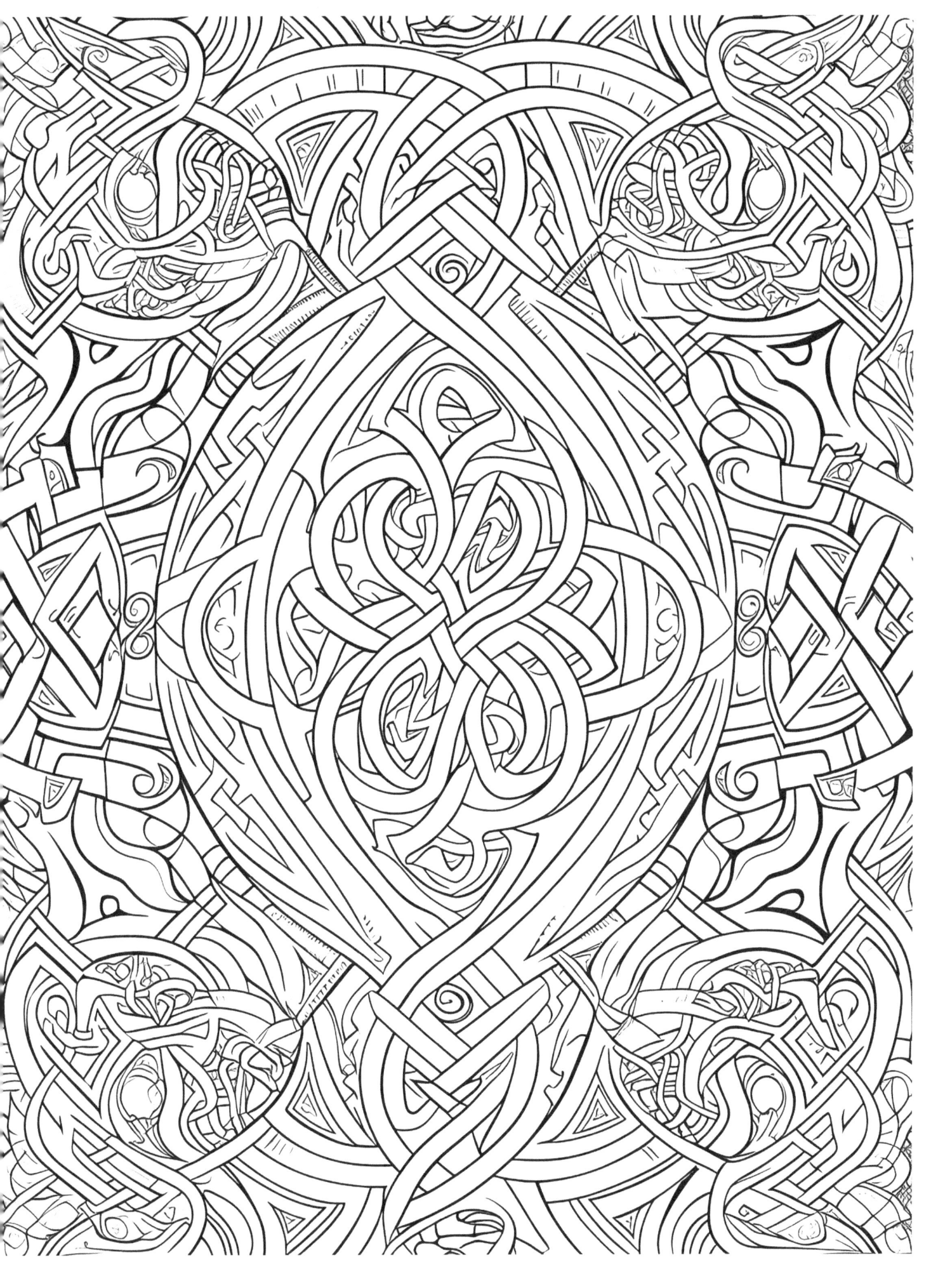

The Big Book of Mandalas & Patterns Coloring Pages
Variety Collection 1

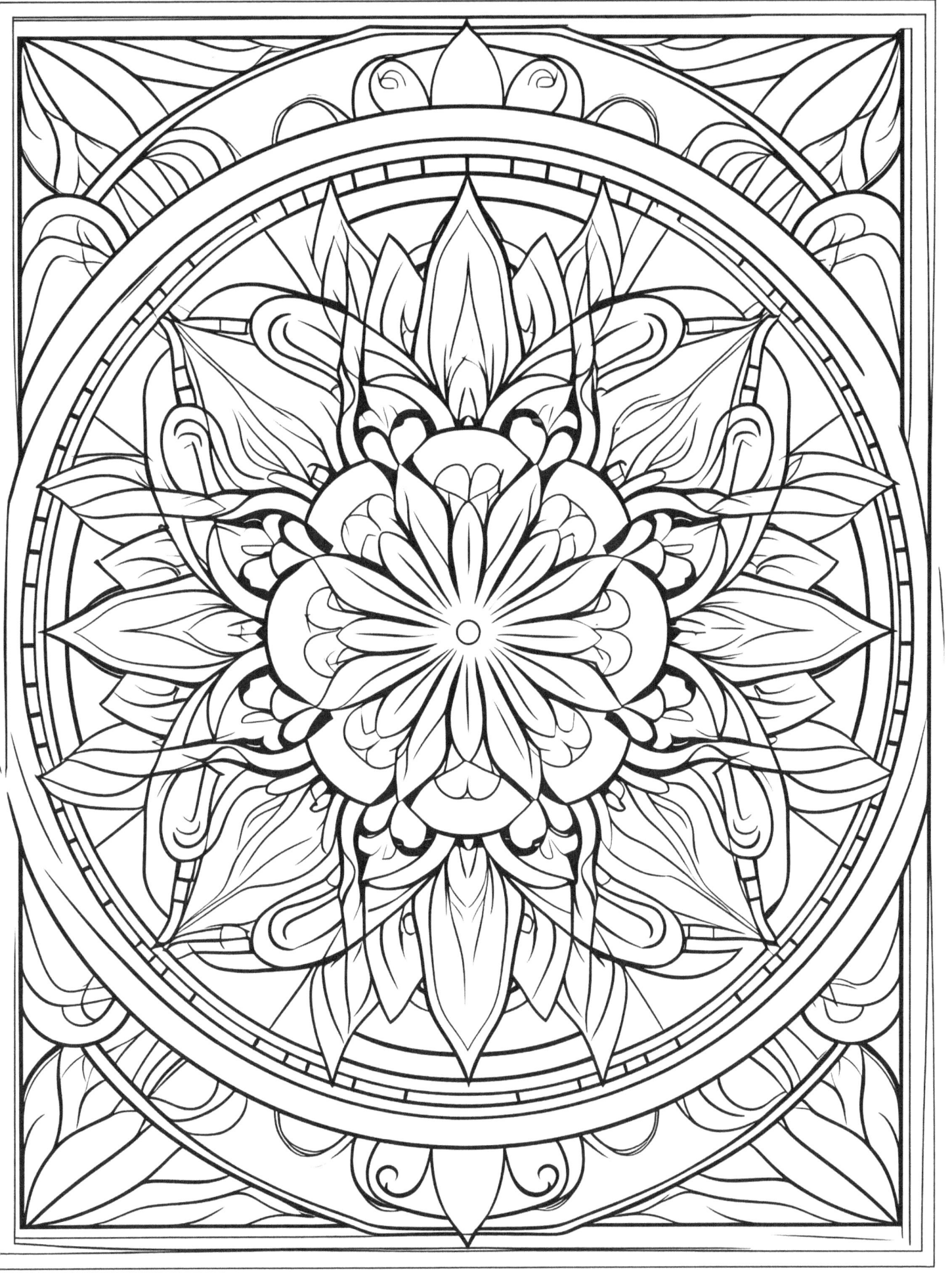

The Big Book of Mandalas & Patterns Coloring Pages
Variety Collection 1

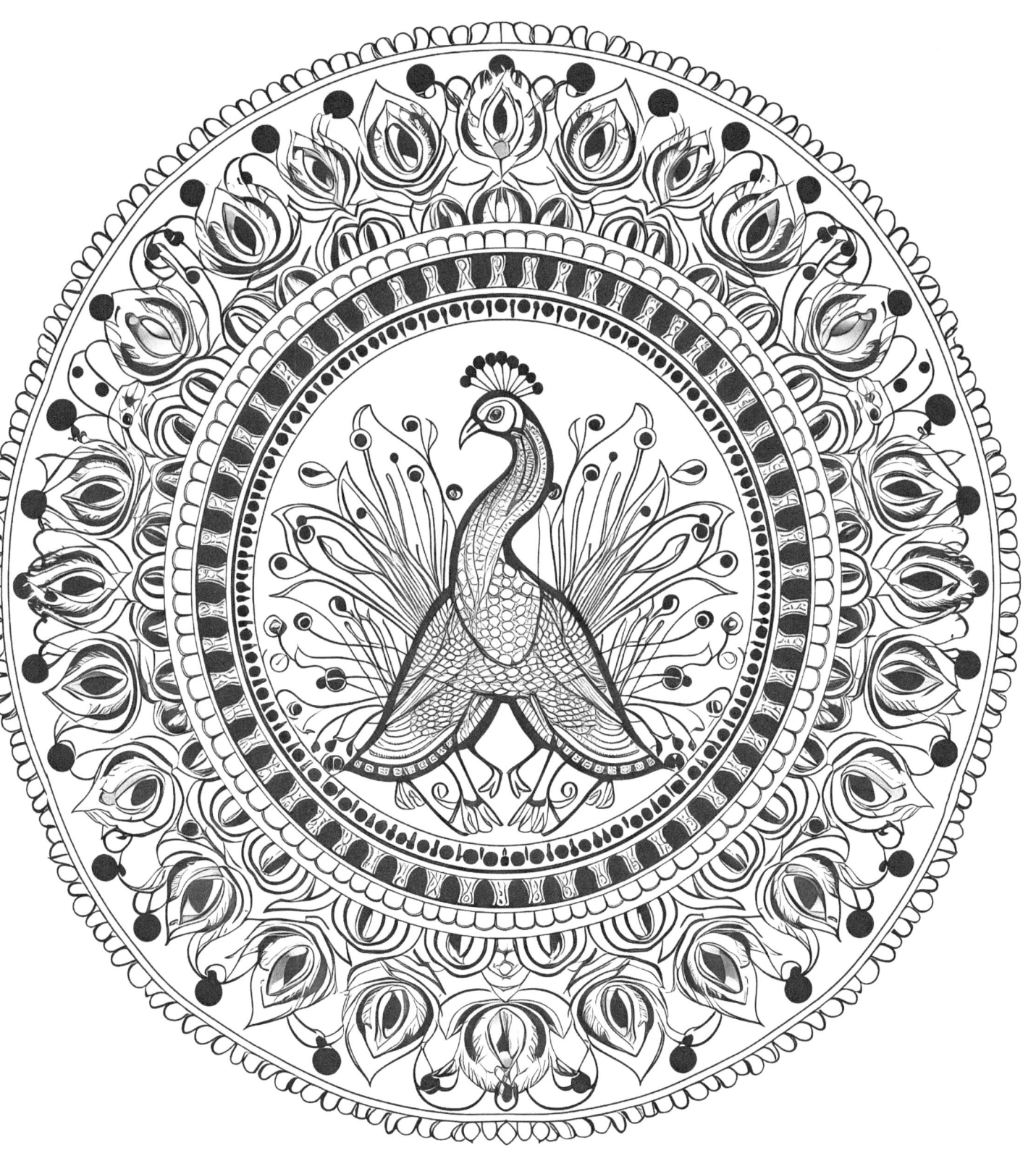

The Big Book of Mandalas & Patterns Coloring Pages
Variety Collection 1

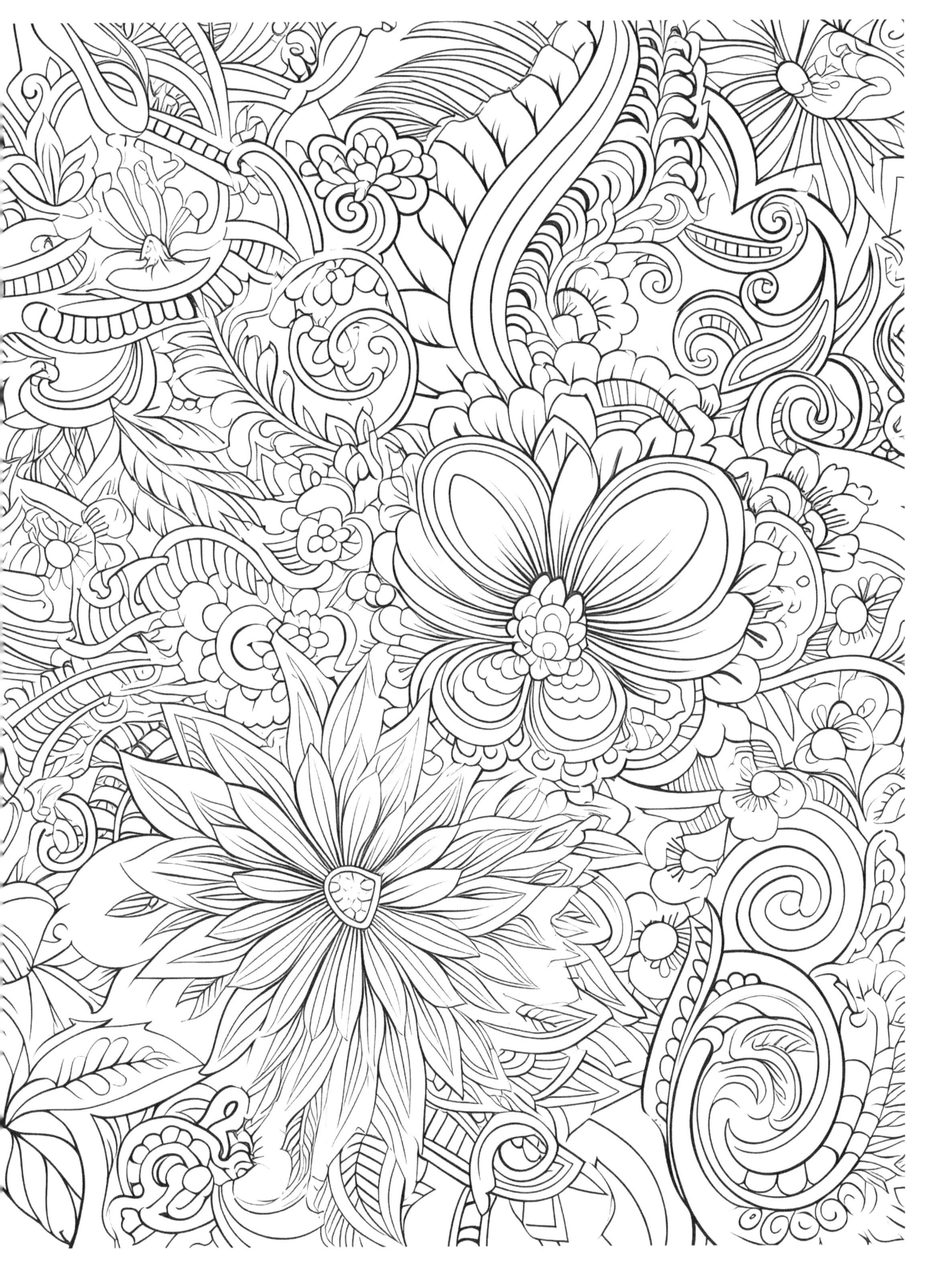

The Big Book of Mandalas & Patterns Coloring Pages
Variety Collection 1

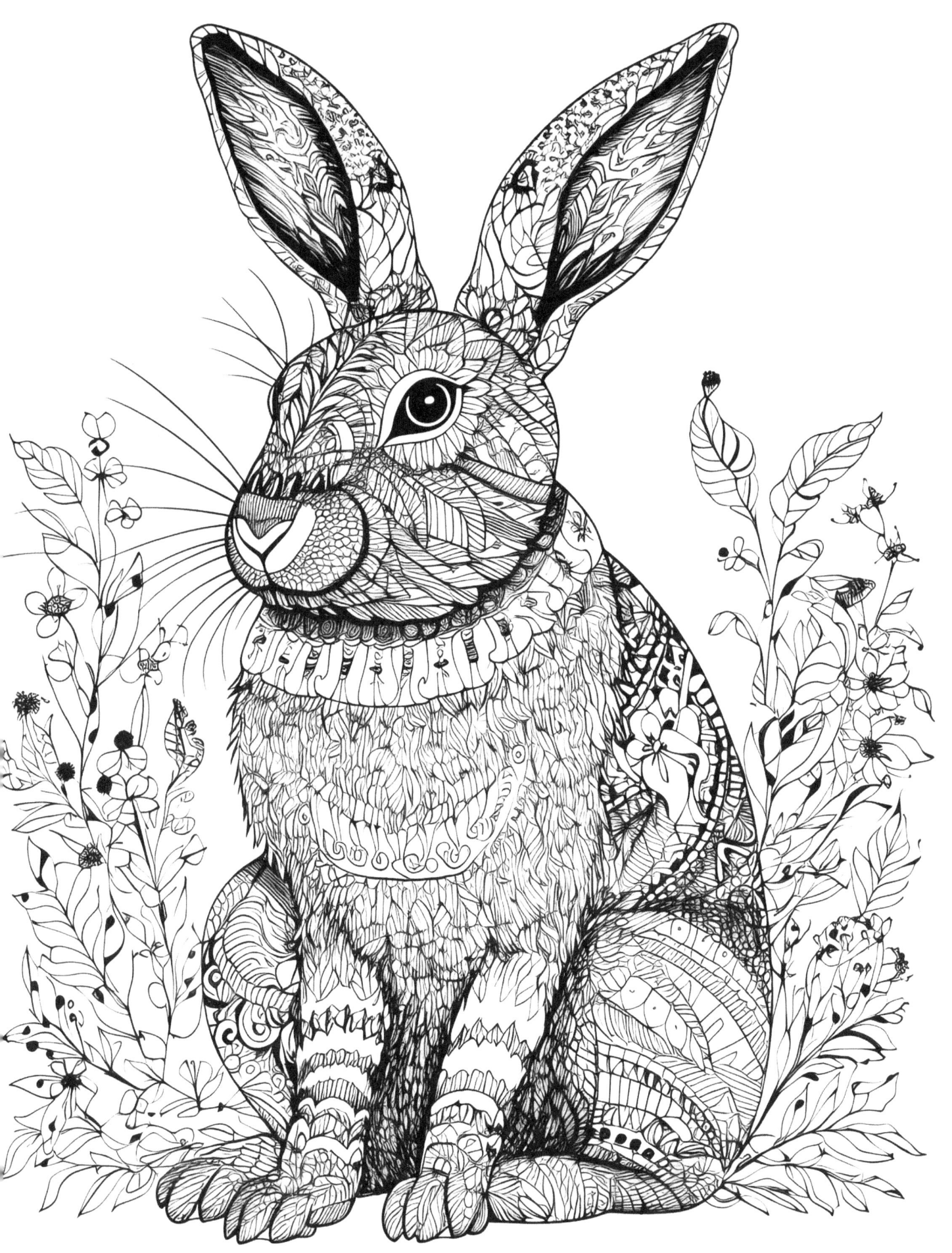

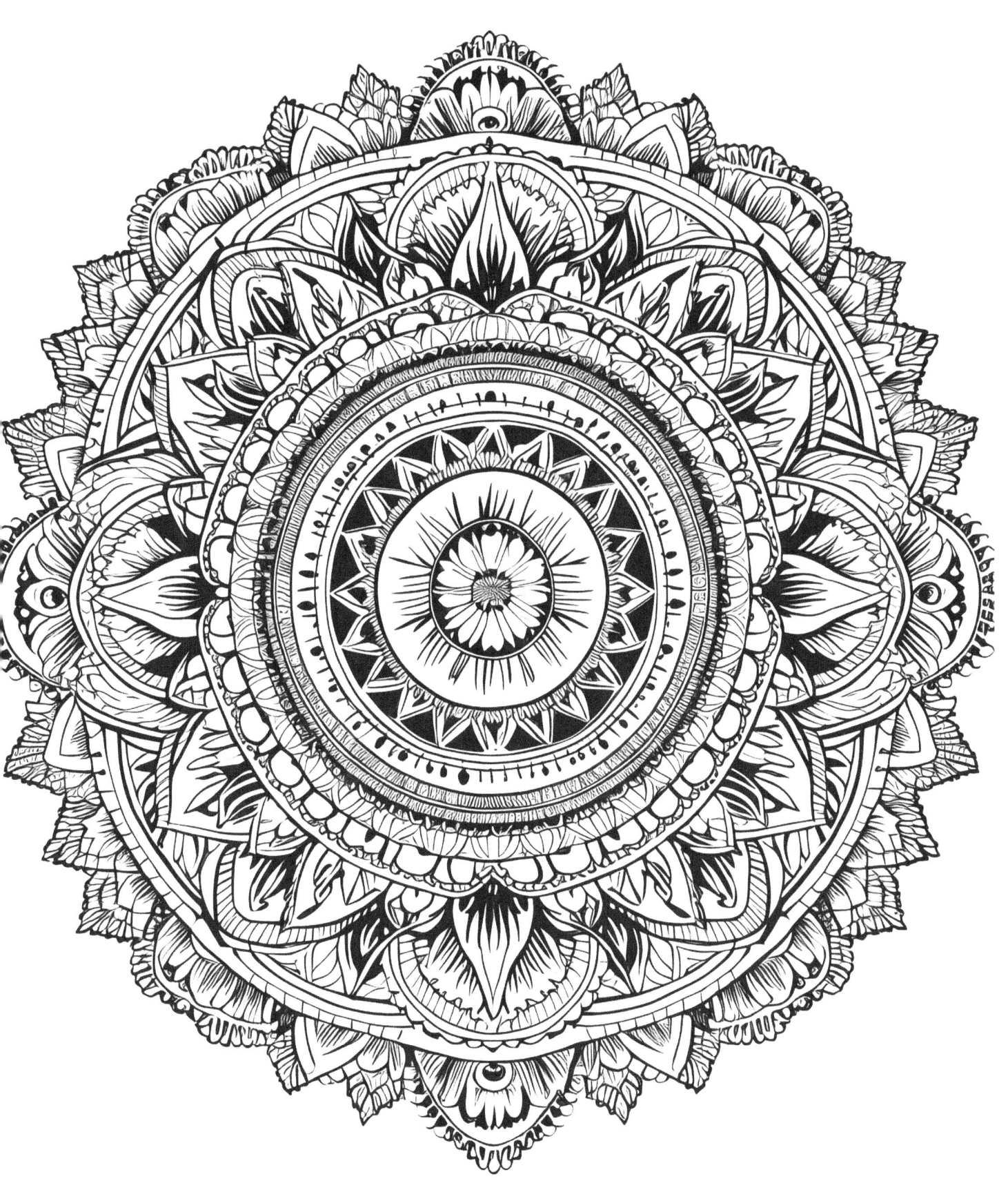

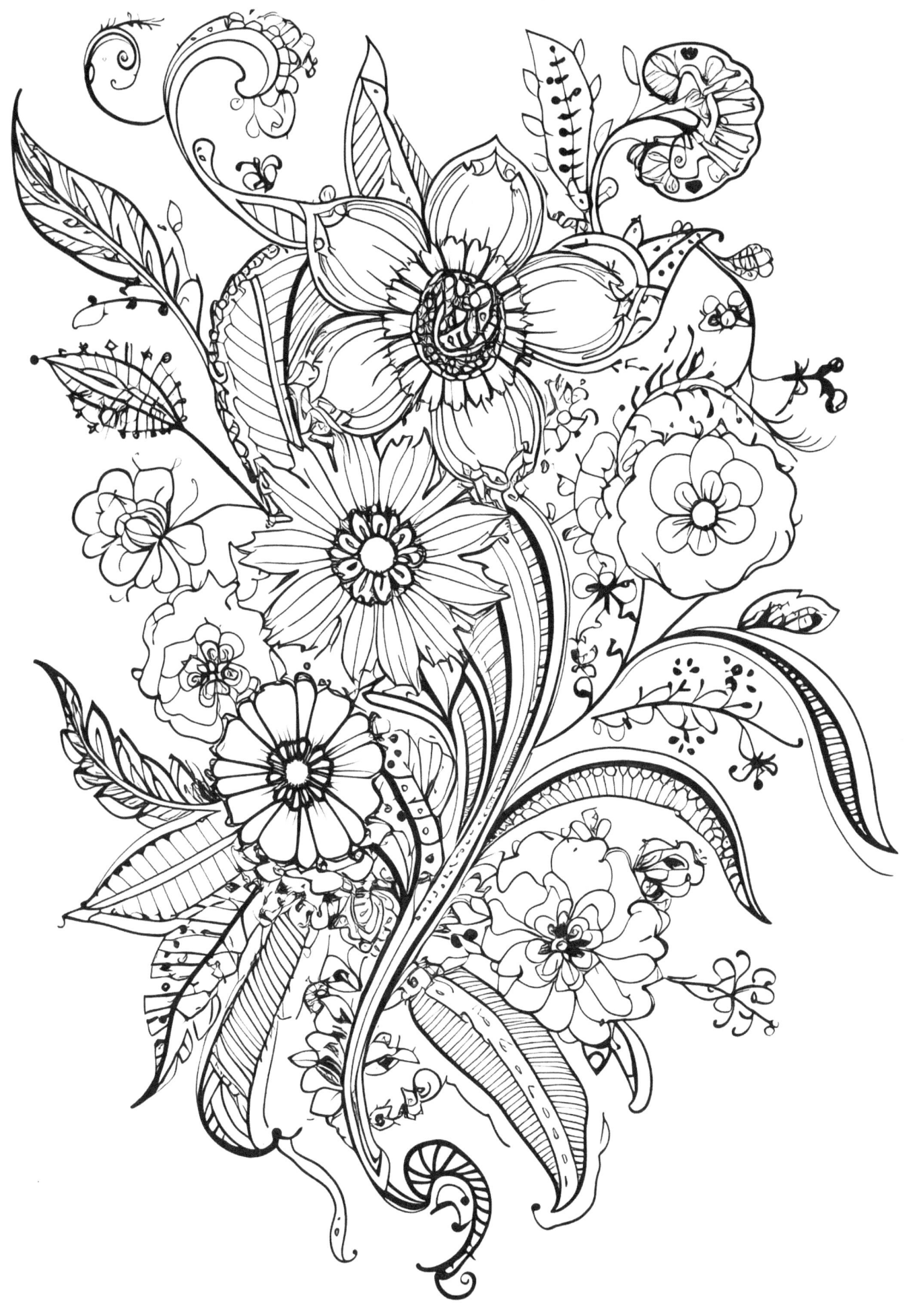

The Big Book of Mandalas & Patterns Coloring Pages
Variety Collection 1

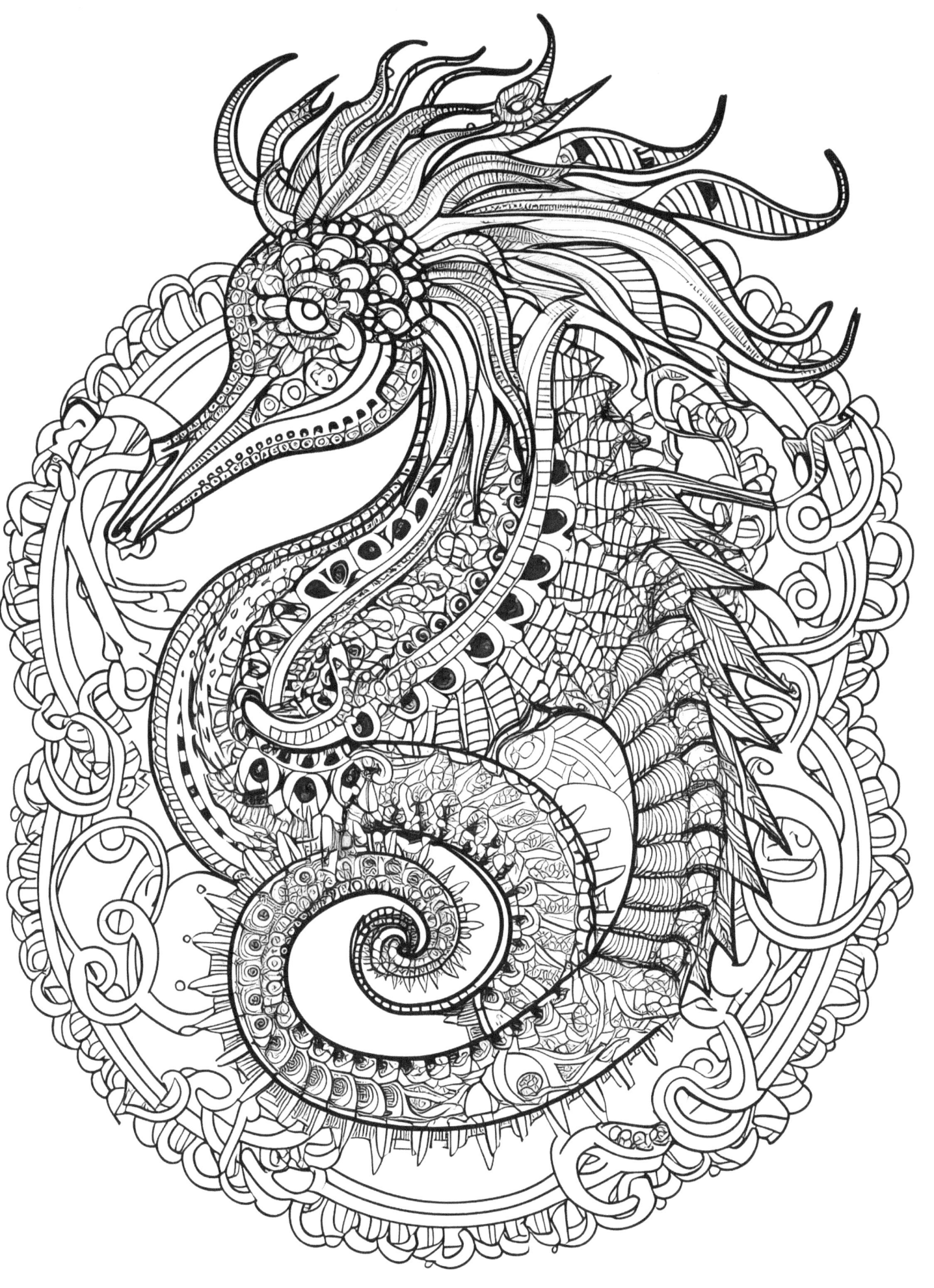

The Big Book of Mandalas & Patterns Coloring Pages
Variety Collection 1

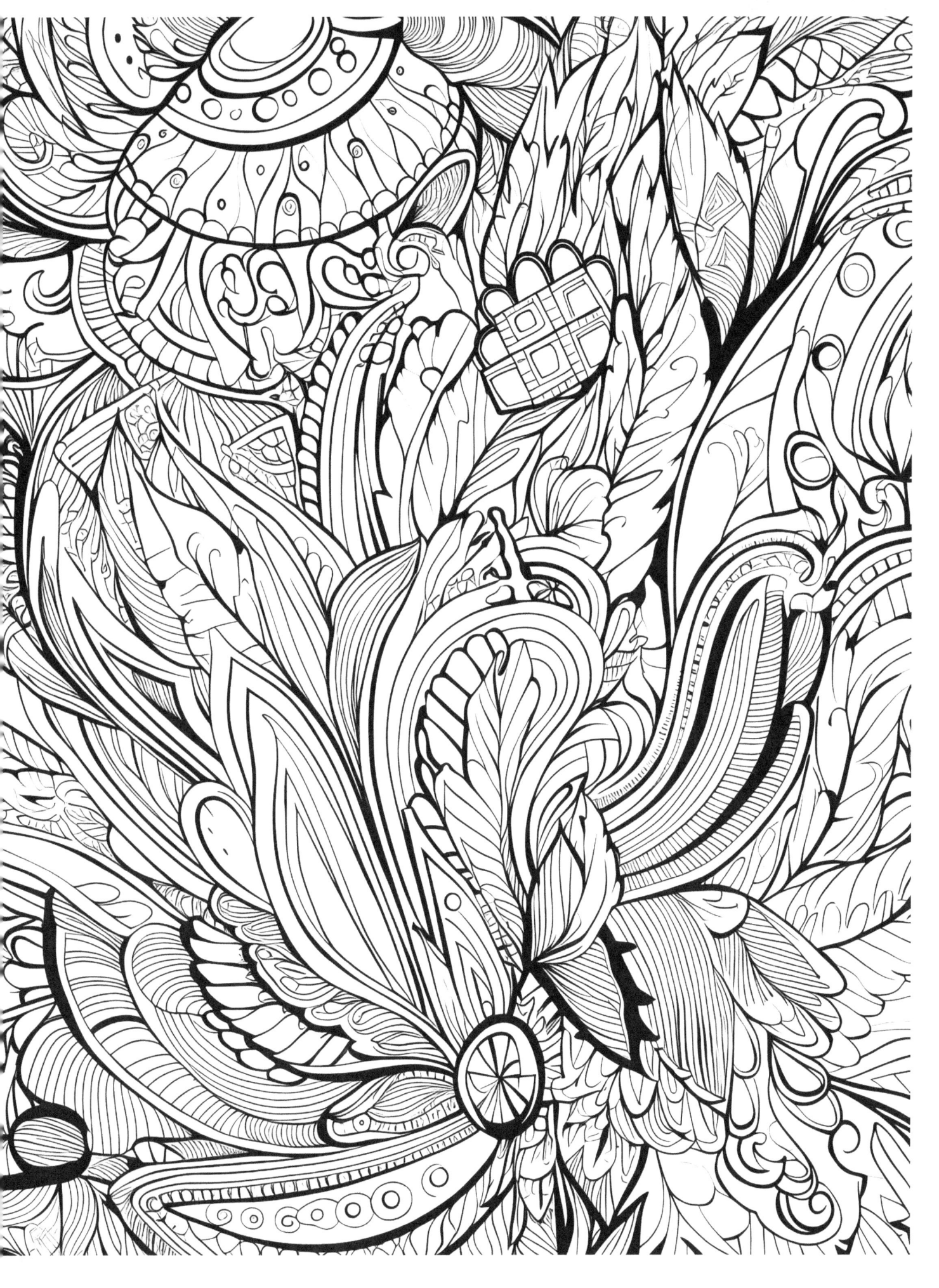

The Big Book of Mandalas & Patterns Coloring Pages
Variety Collection 1

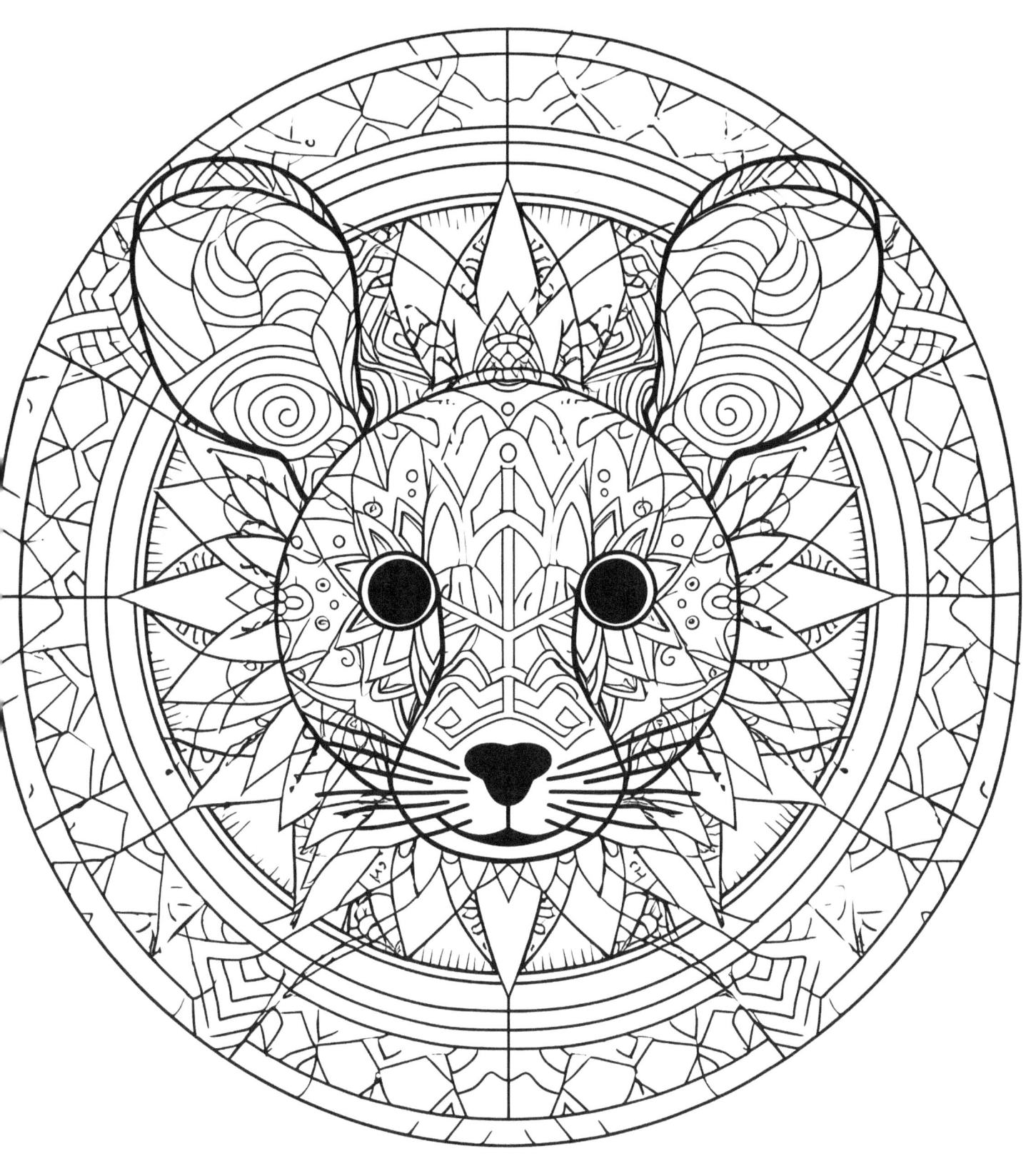

The Big Book of Mandalas & Patterns Coloring Pages
Variety Collection 1

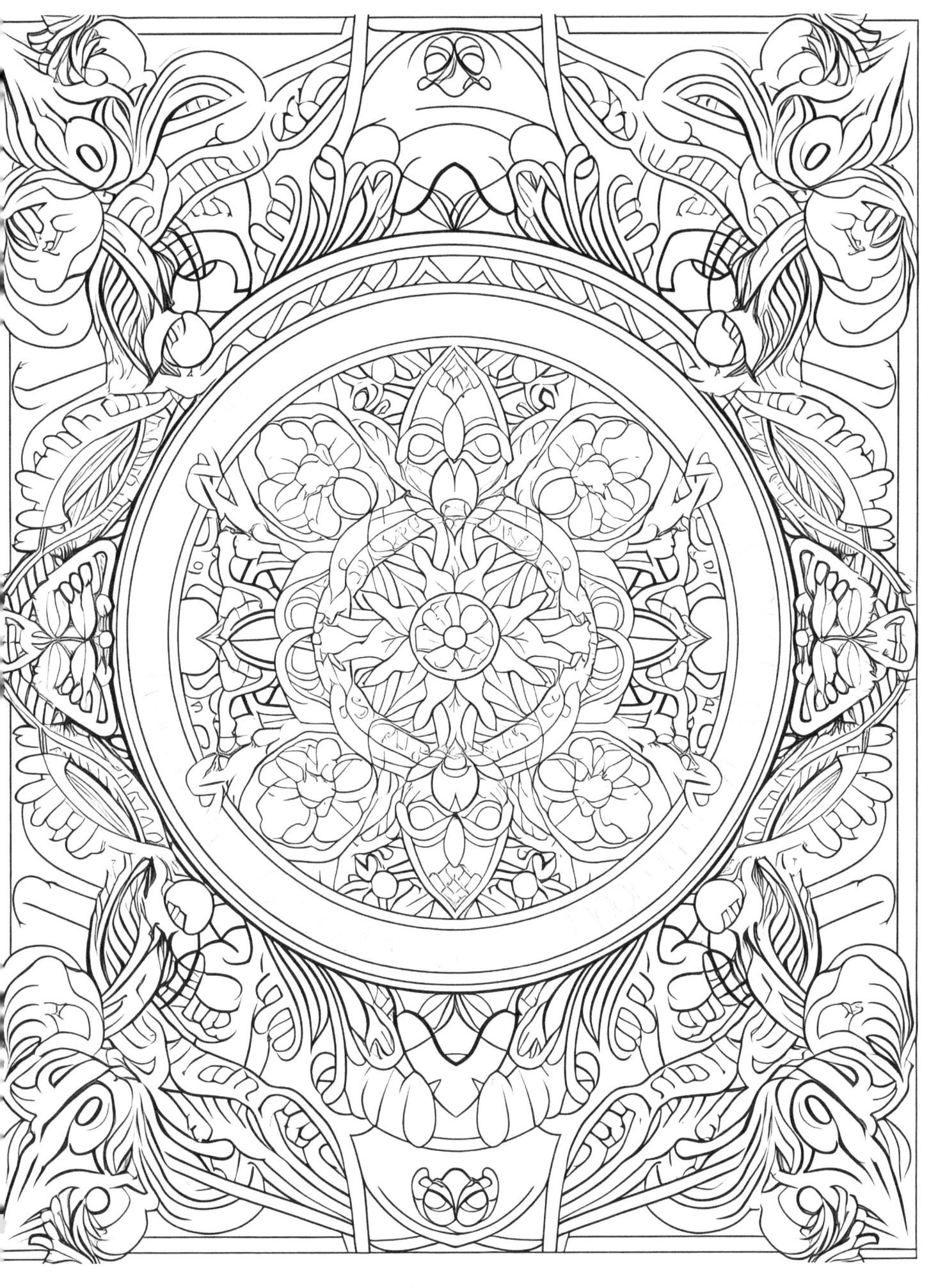

The Big Book of Mandalas & Patterns Coloring Pages
Variety Collection 1

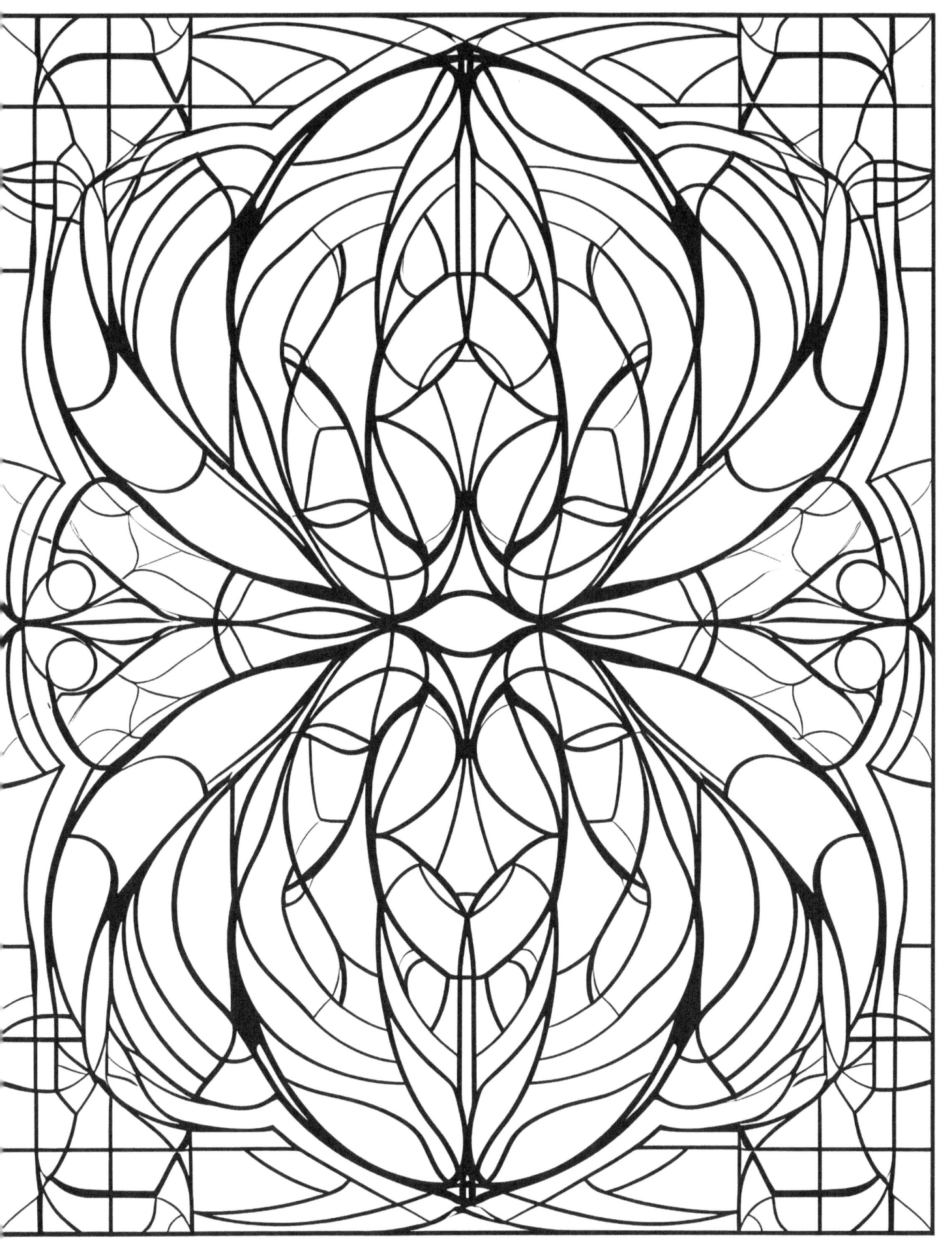

The Big Book of Mandalas & Patterns Coloring Pages
Variety Collection 1

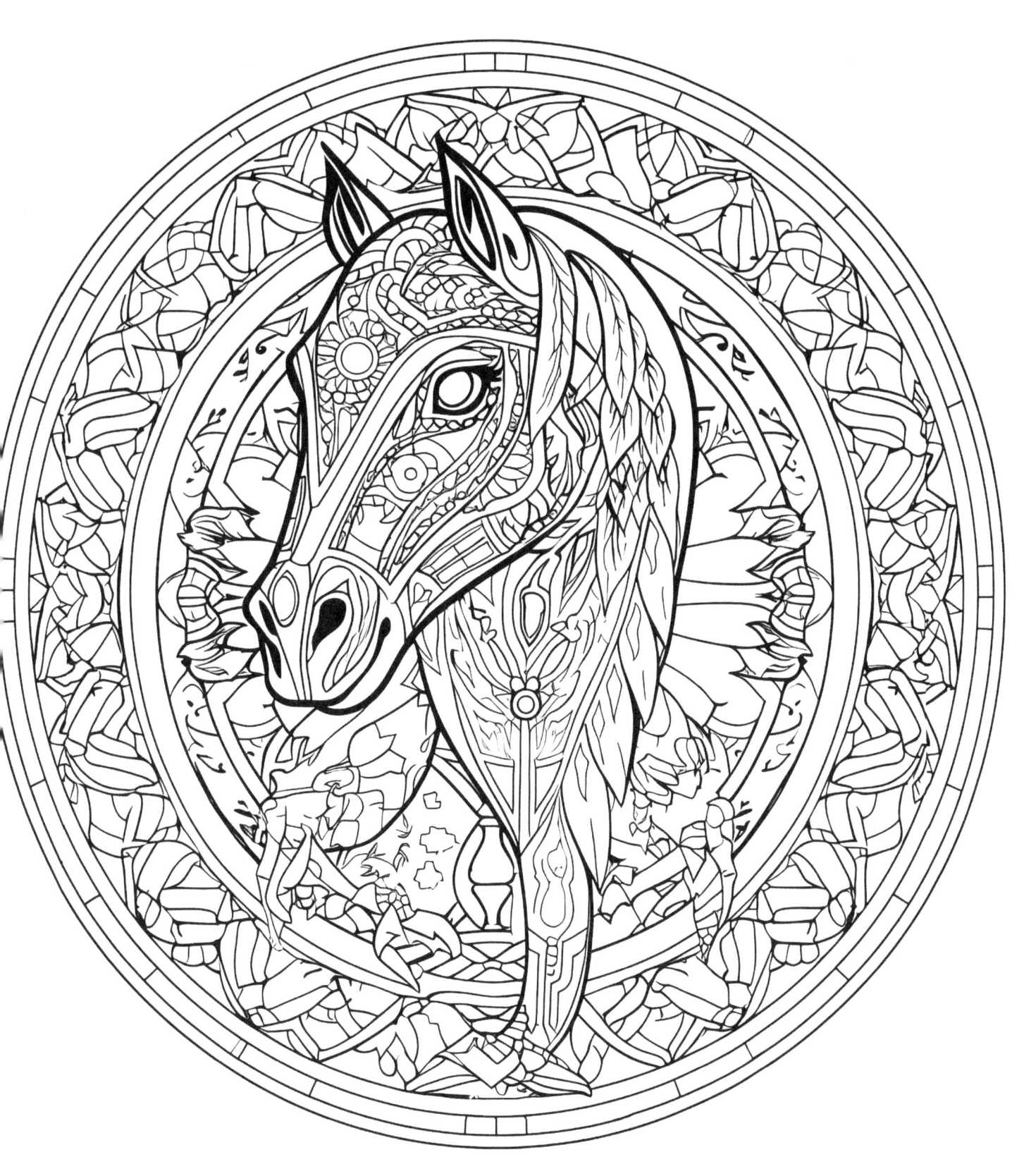

The Big Book of Mandalas & Patterns Coloring Pages
Variety Collection 1

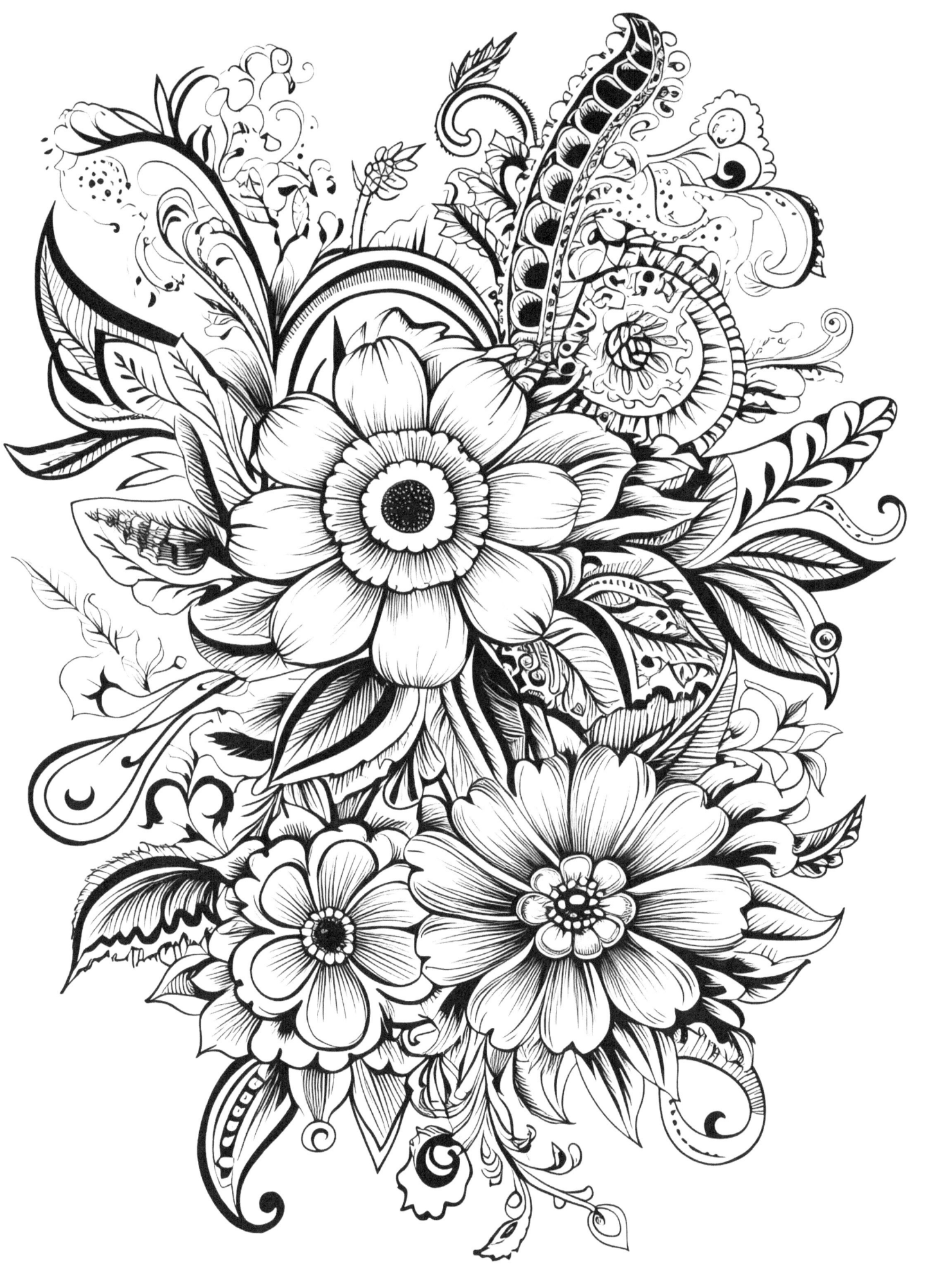

The Big Book of Mandalas & Patterns Coloring Pages
Variety Collection 1

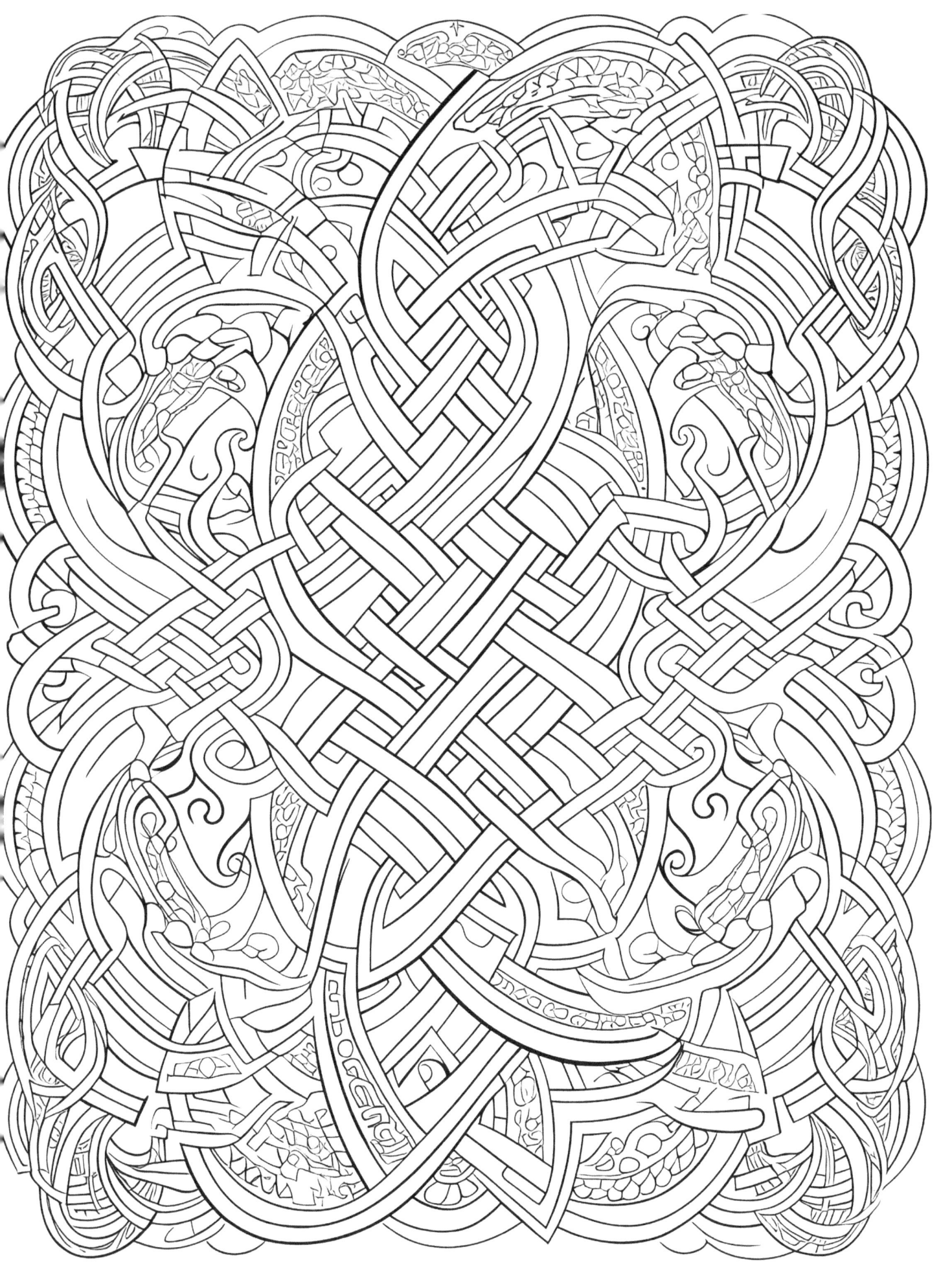

The Big Book of Mandalas & Patterns Coloring Pages
Variety Collection 1

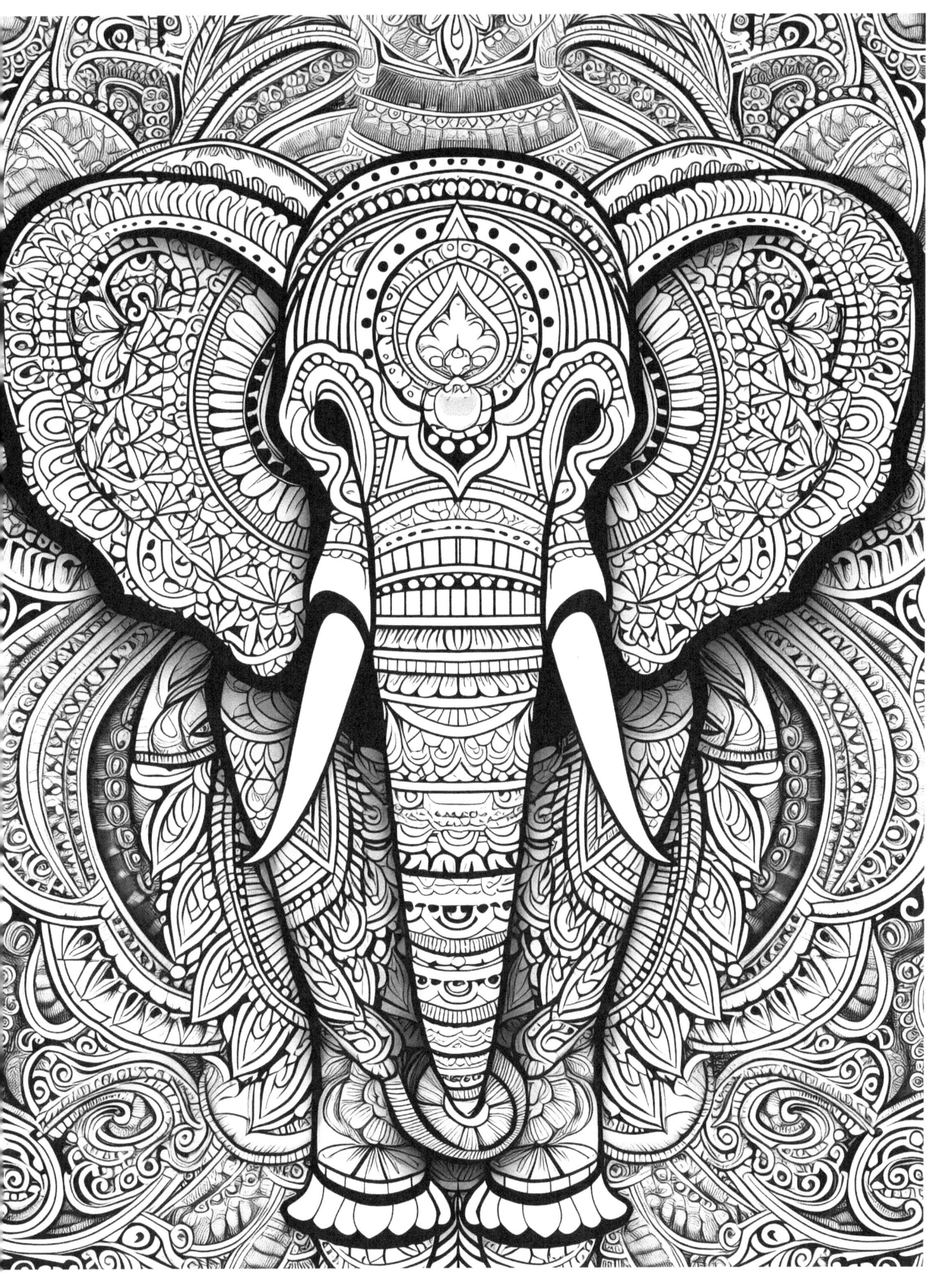

The Big Book of Mandalas & Patterns Coloring Pages
Variety Collection 1

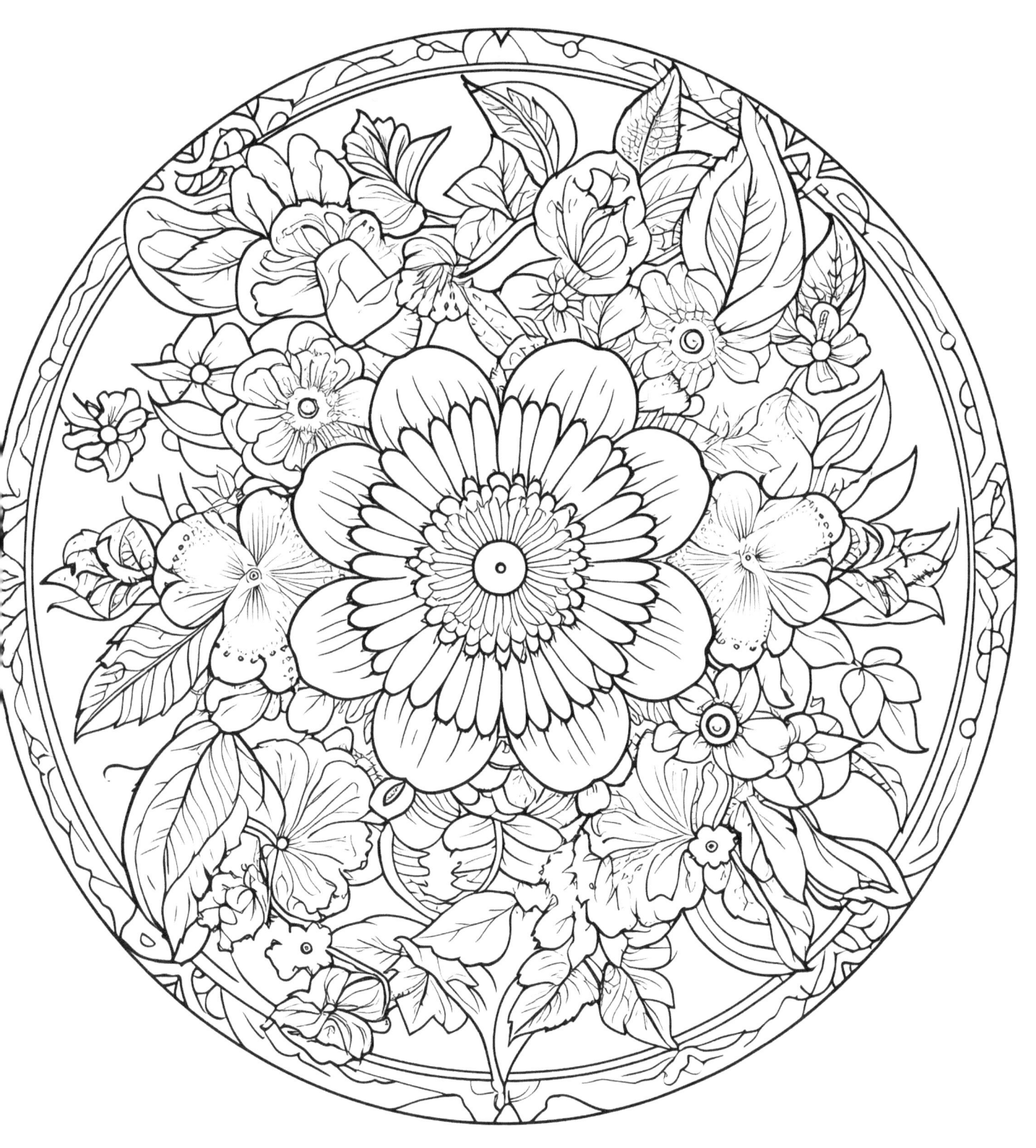

The Big Book of Mandalas & Patterns Coloring Pages
Variety Collection 1

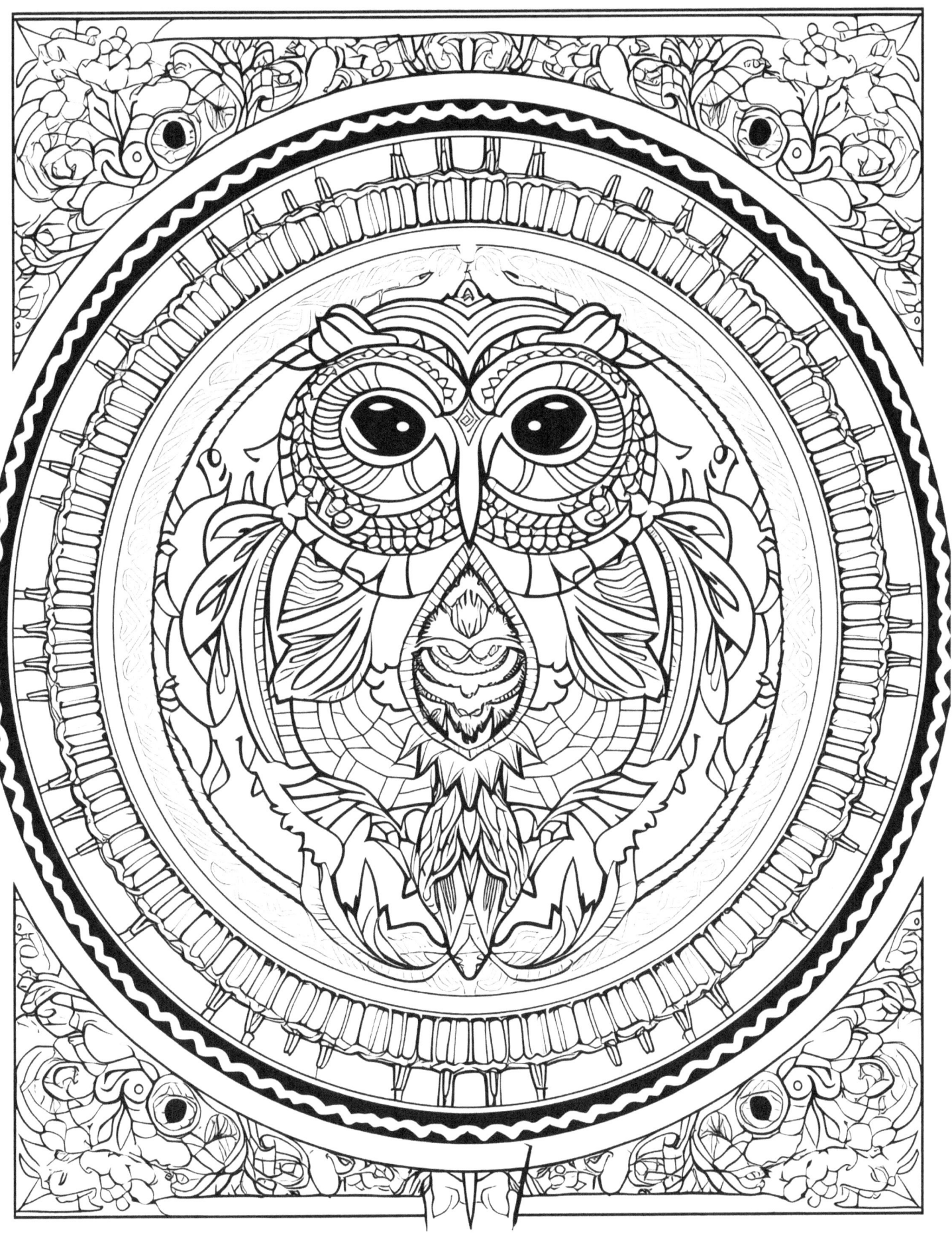

The Big Book of Mandalas & Patterns Coloring Pages
Variety Collection 1

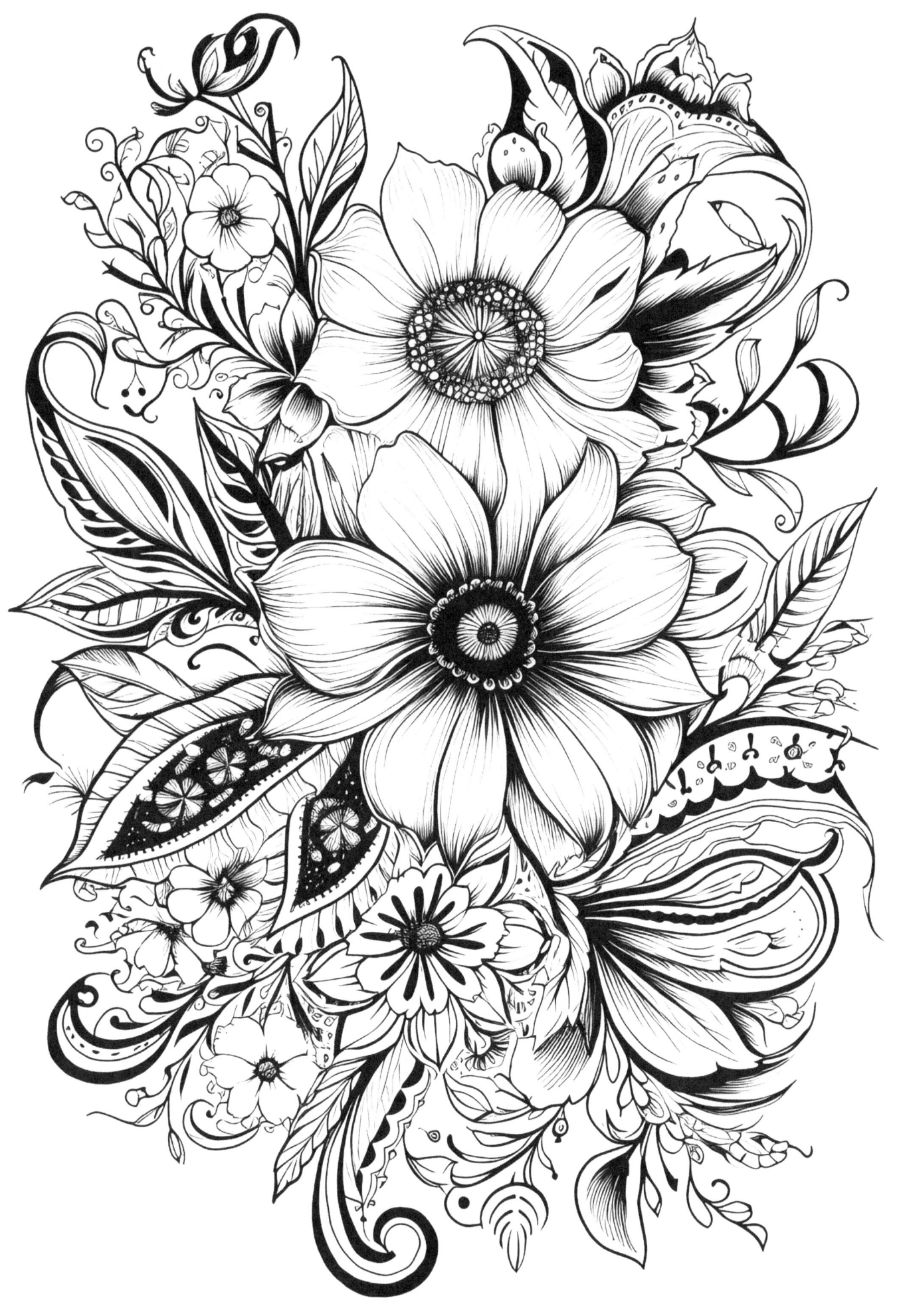

The Big Book of Mandalas & Patterns Coloring Pages
Variety Collection 1

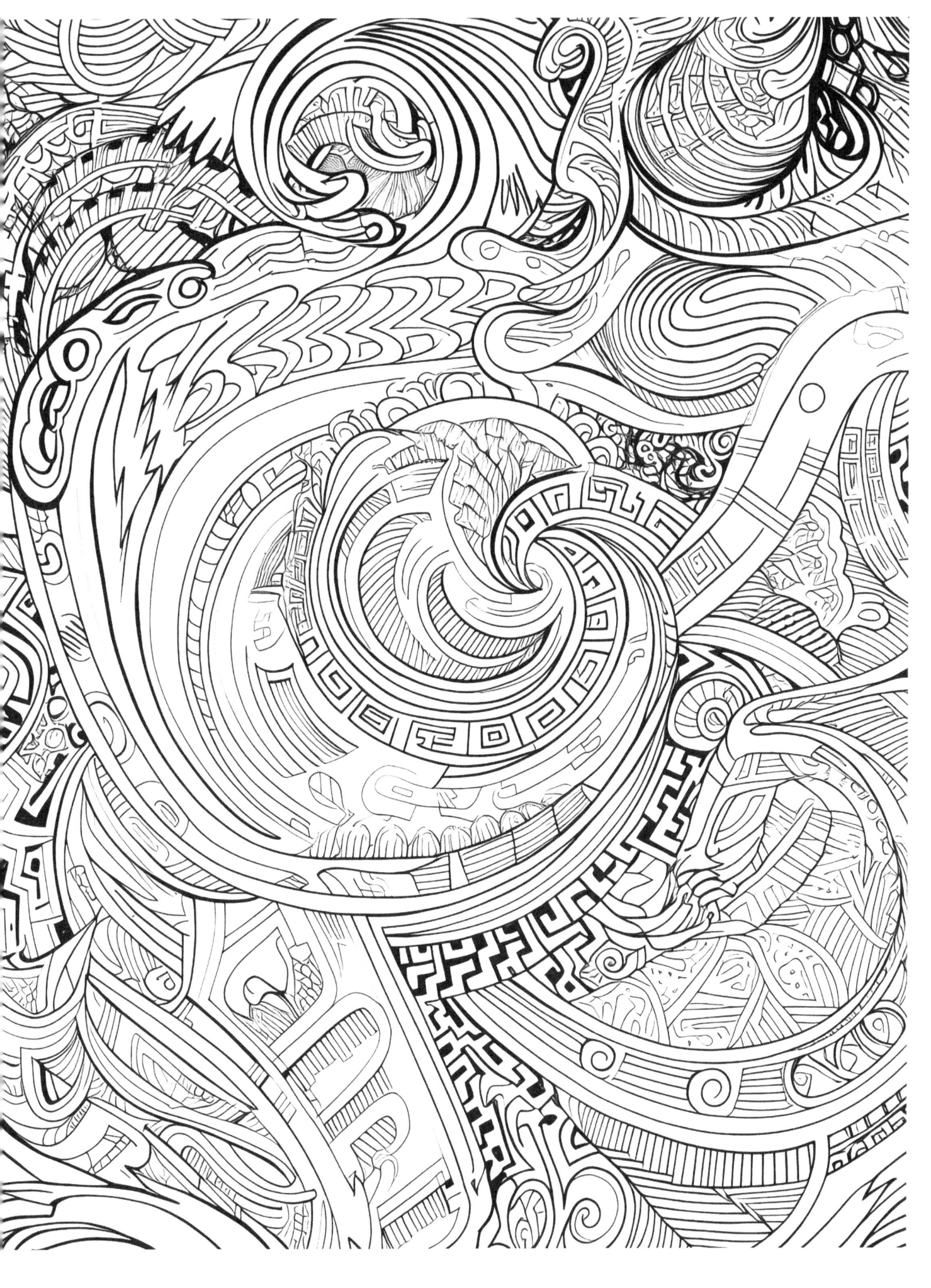

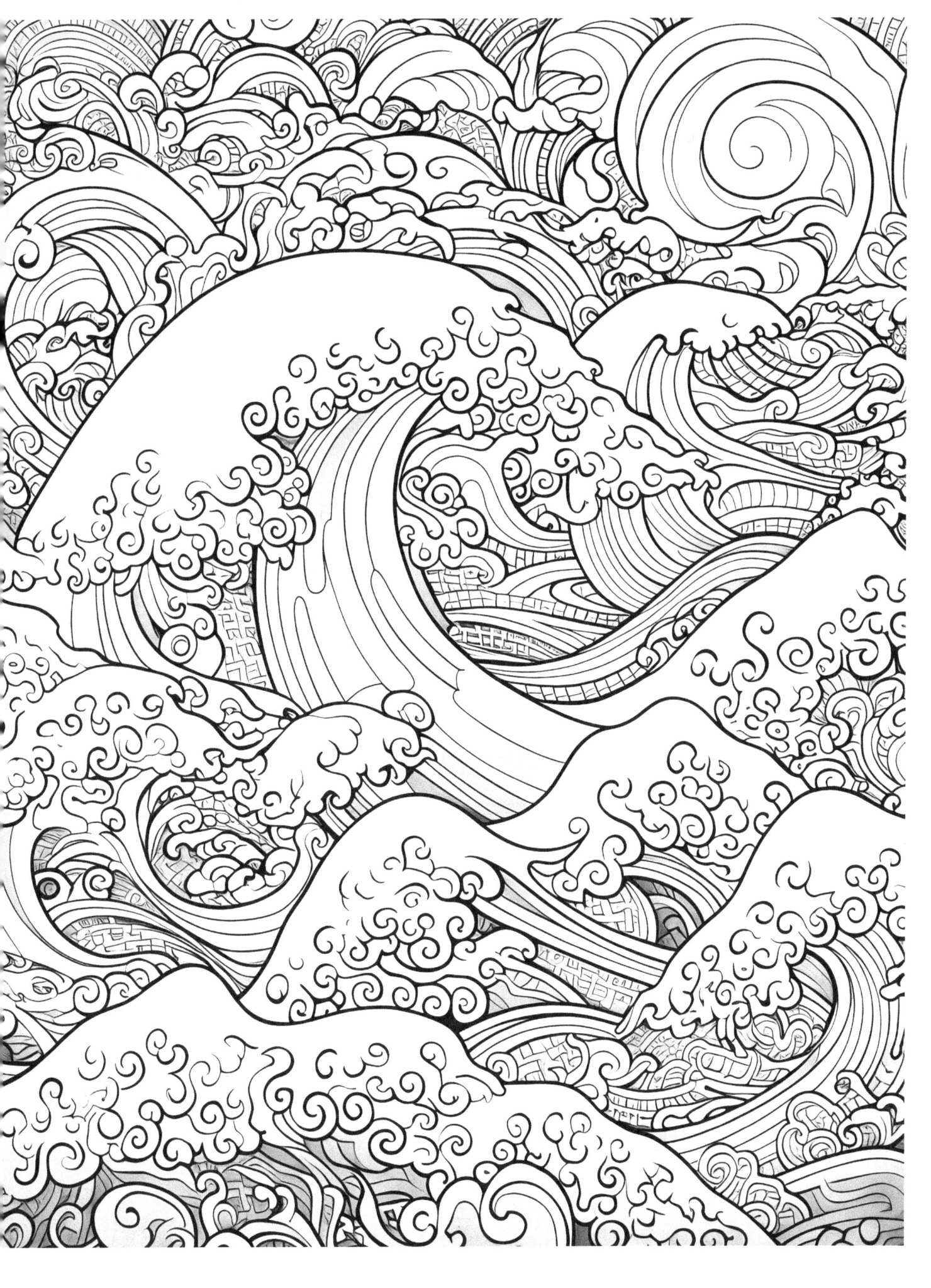

The Big Book of Mandalas & Patterns Coloring Pages
Variety Collection 1

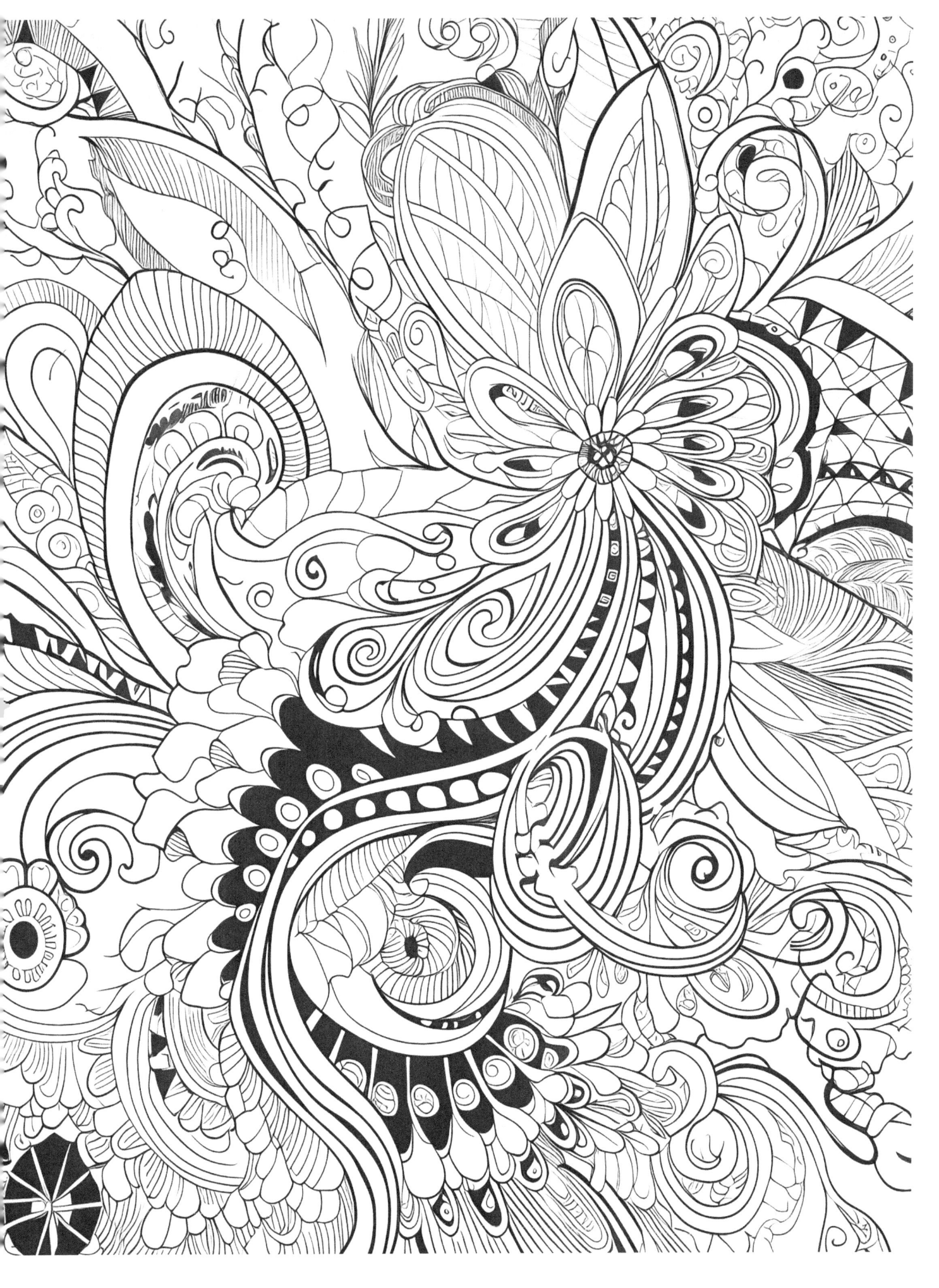

The Big Book of Mandalas & Patterns Coloring Pages
Variety Collection 1

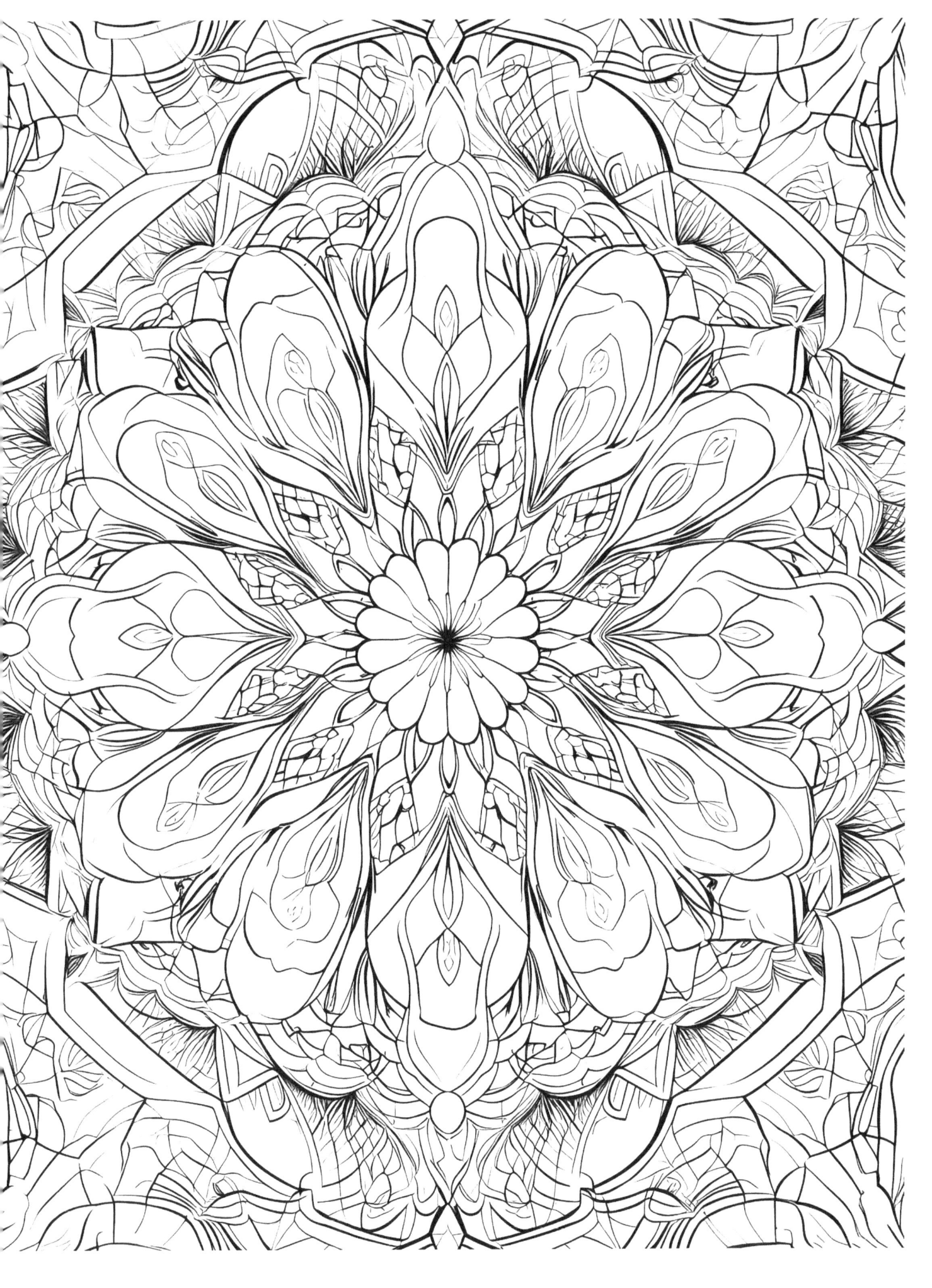

The Big Book of Mandalas & Patterns Coloring Pages
Variety Collection 1

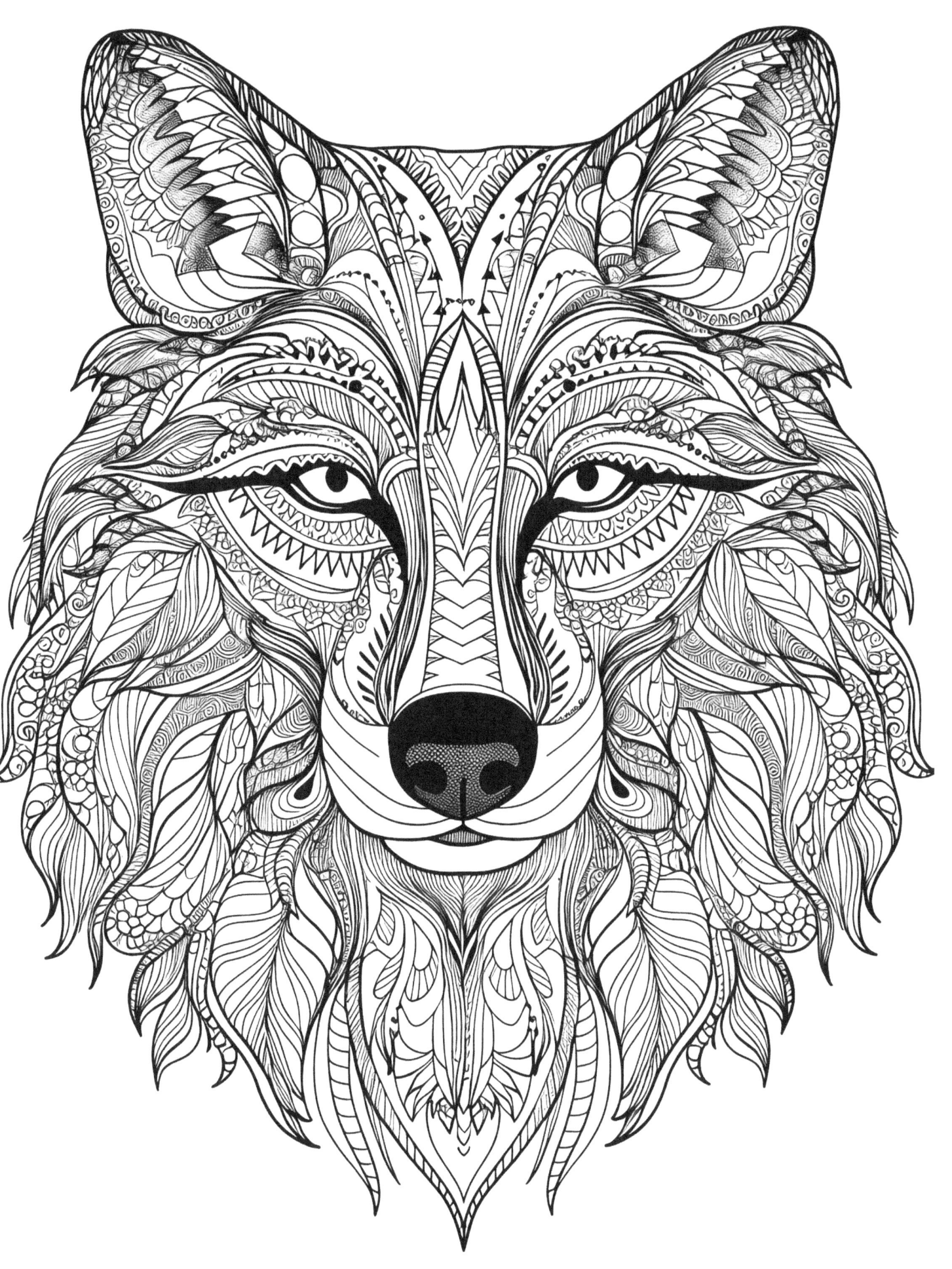

The Big Book of Mandalas & Patterns Coloring Pages
Variety Collection 1

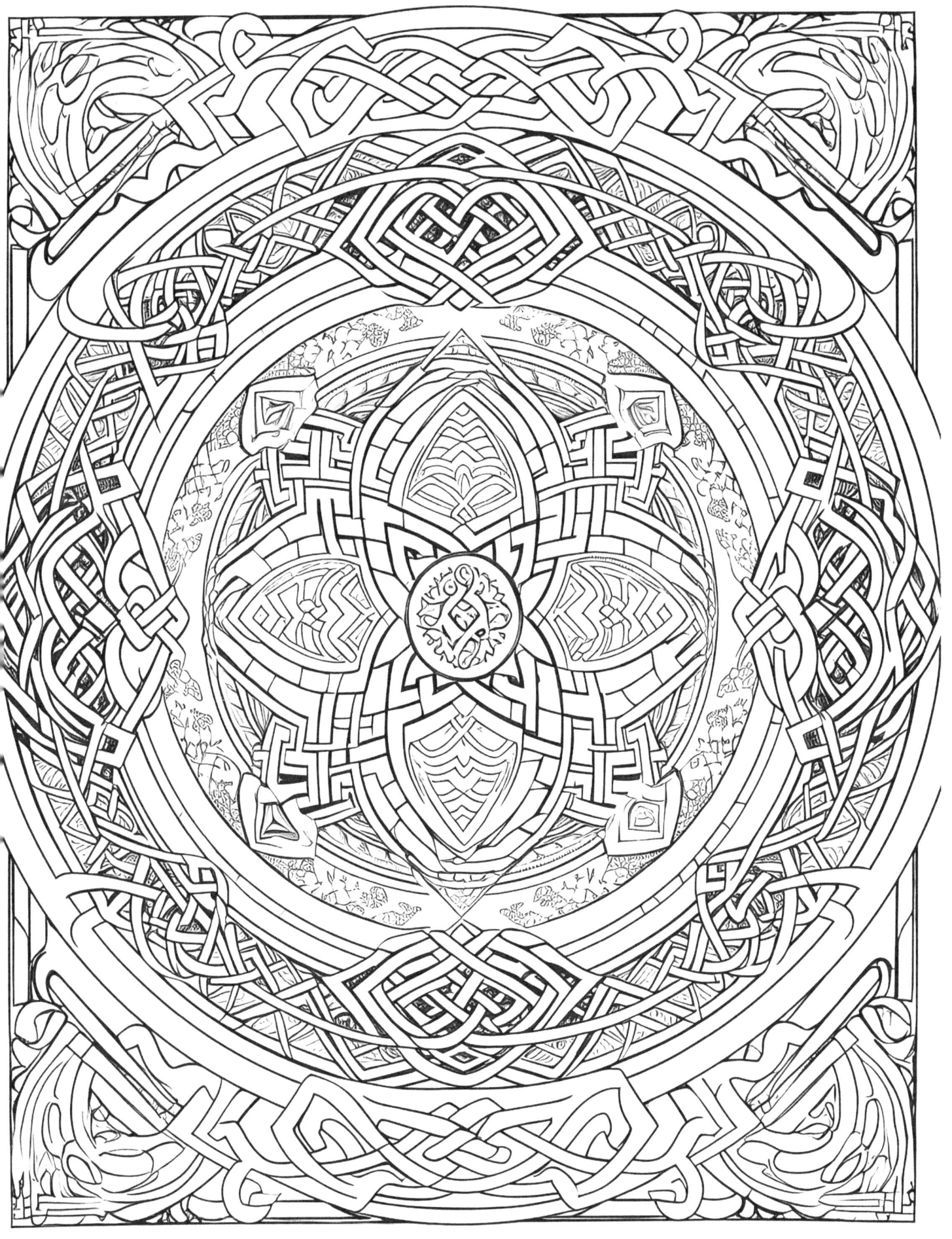

The Big Book of Mandalas & Patterns Coloring Pages
Variety Collection 1

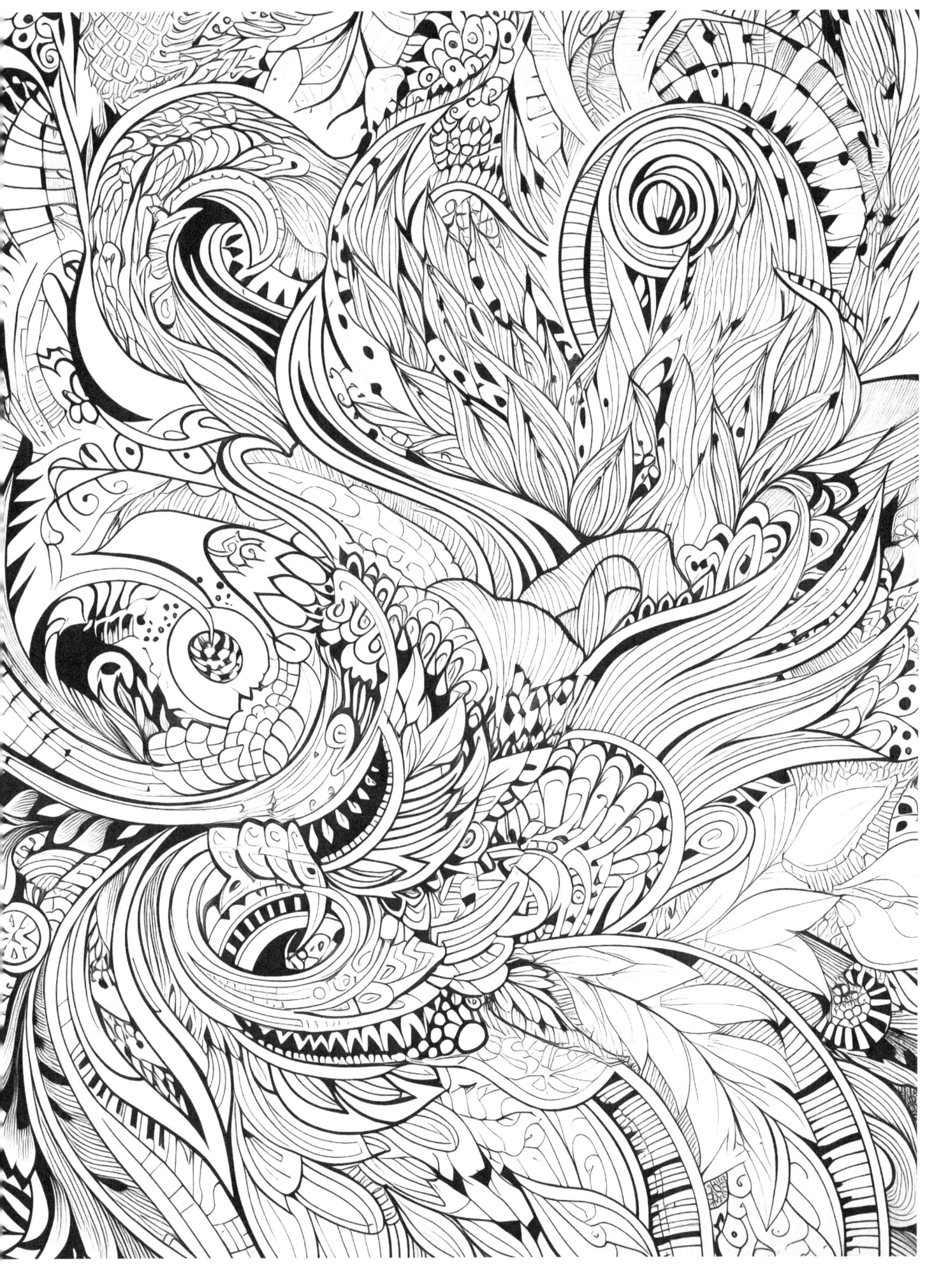

The Big Book of Mandalas & Patterns Coloring Pages
Variety Collection 1

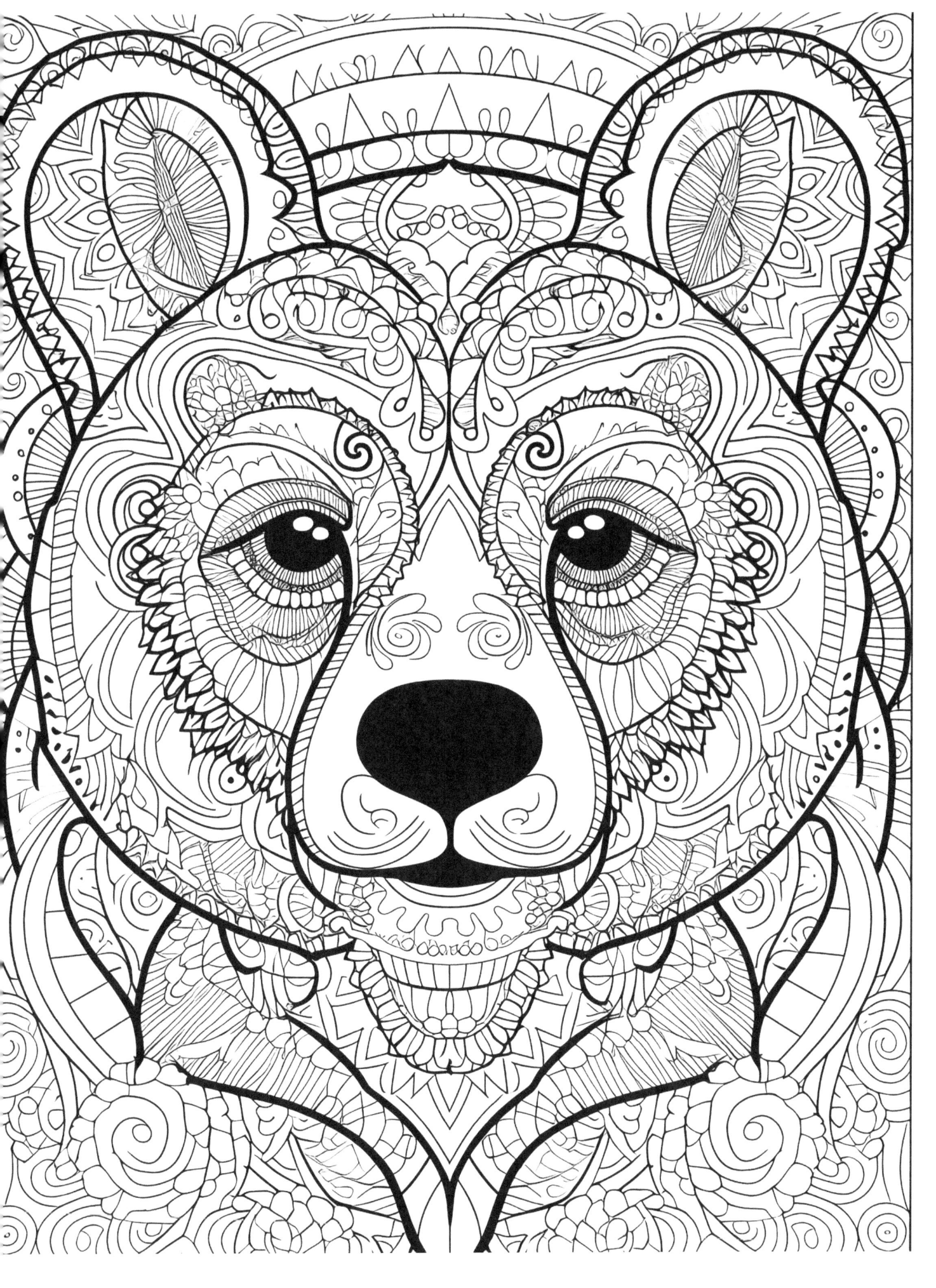

The Big Book of Mandalas & Patterns Coloring Pages
Variety Collection 1

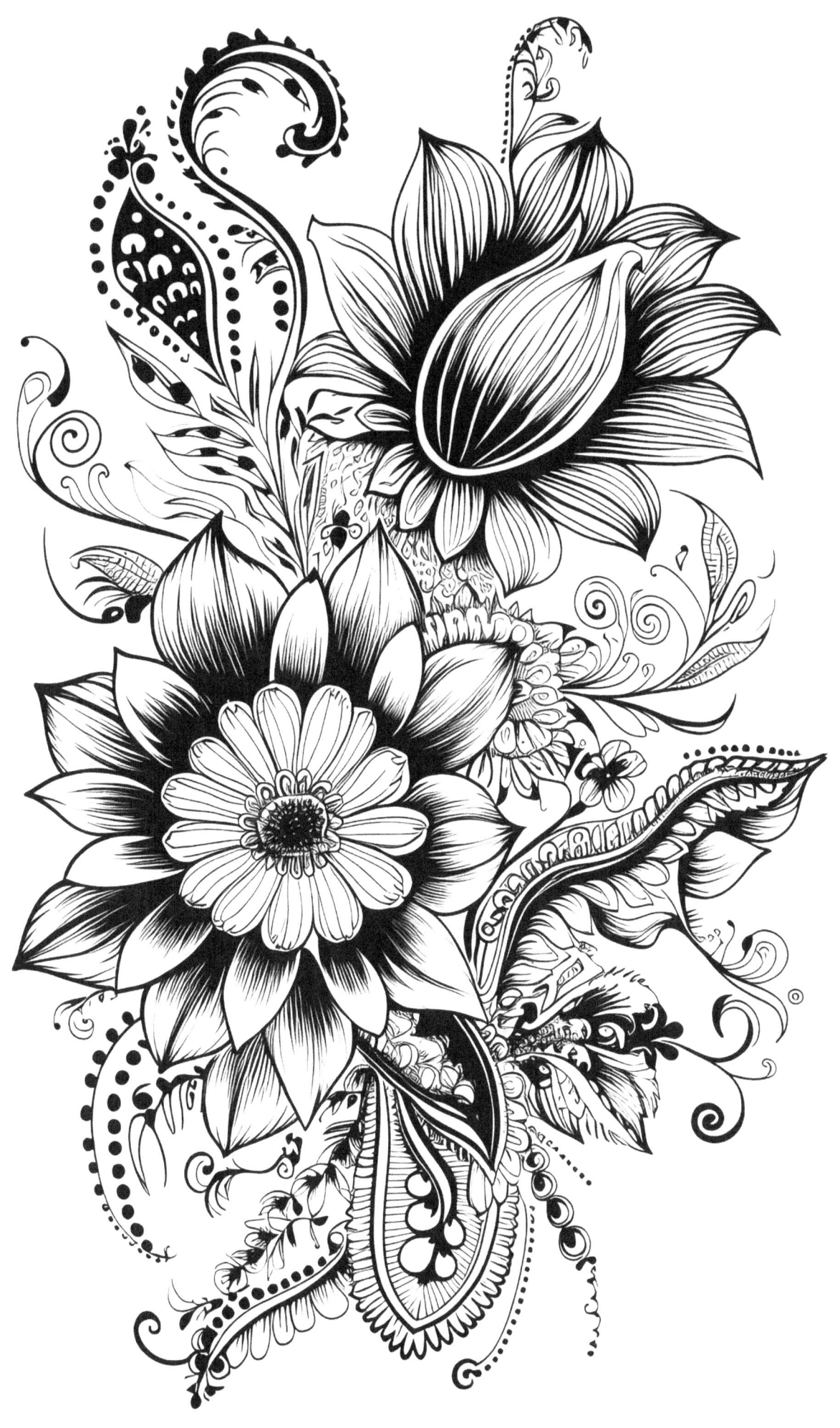

The Big Book of Mandalas & Patterns Coloring Pages
Variety Collection 1

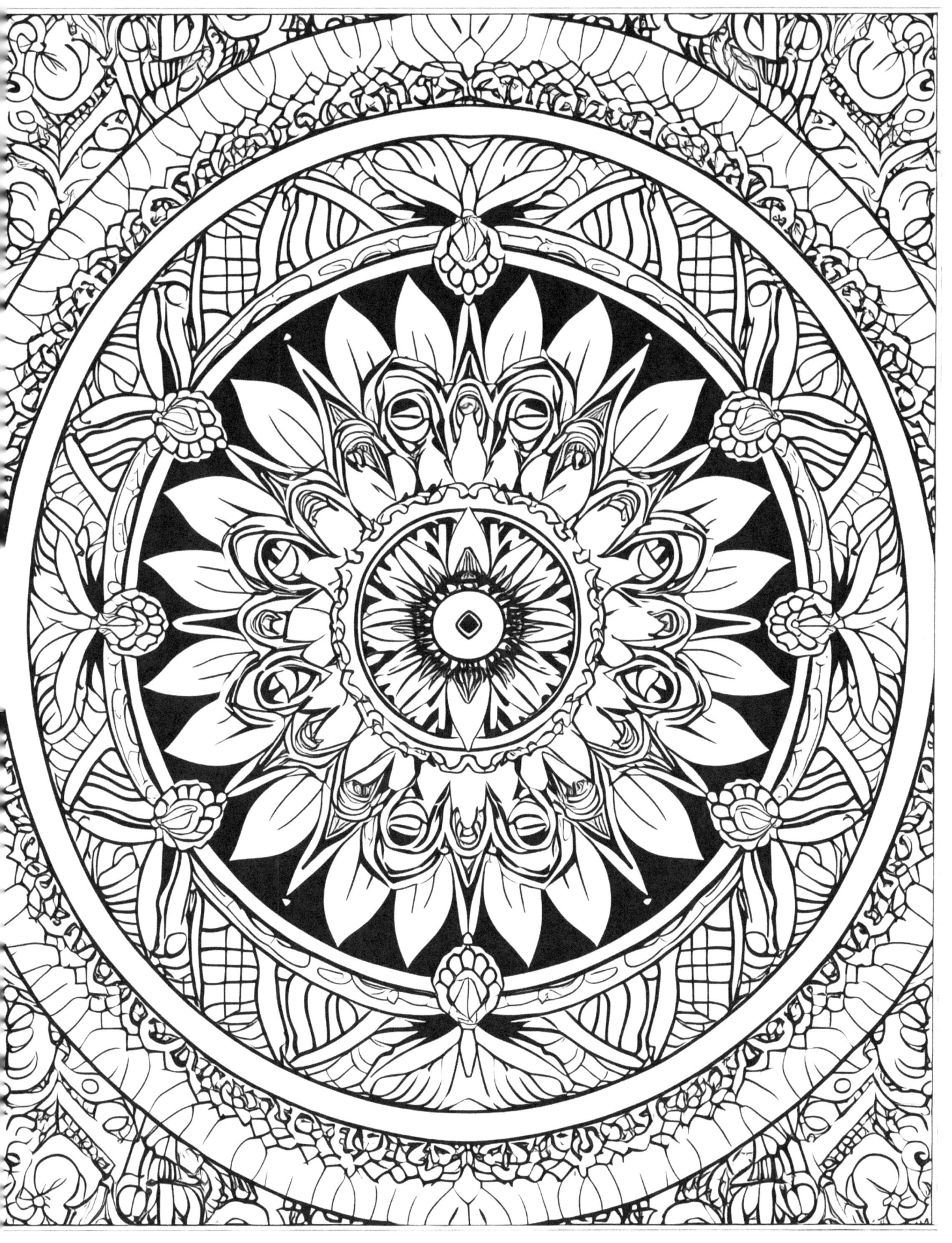

The Big Book of Mandalas & Patterns Coloring Pages
Variety Collection 1

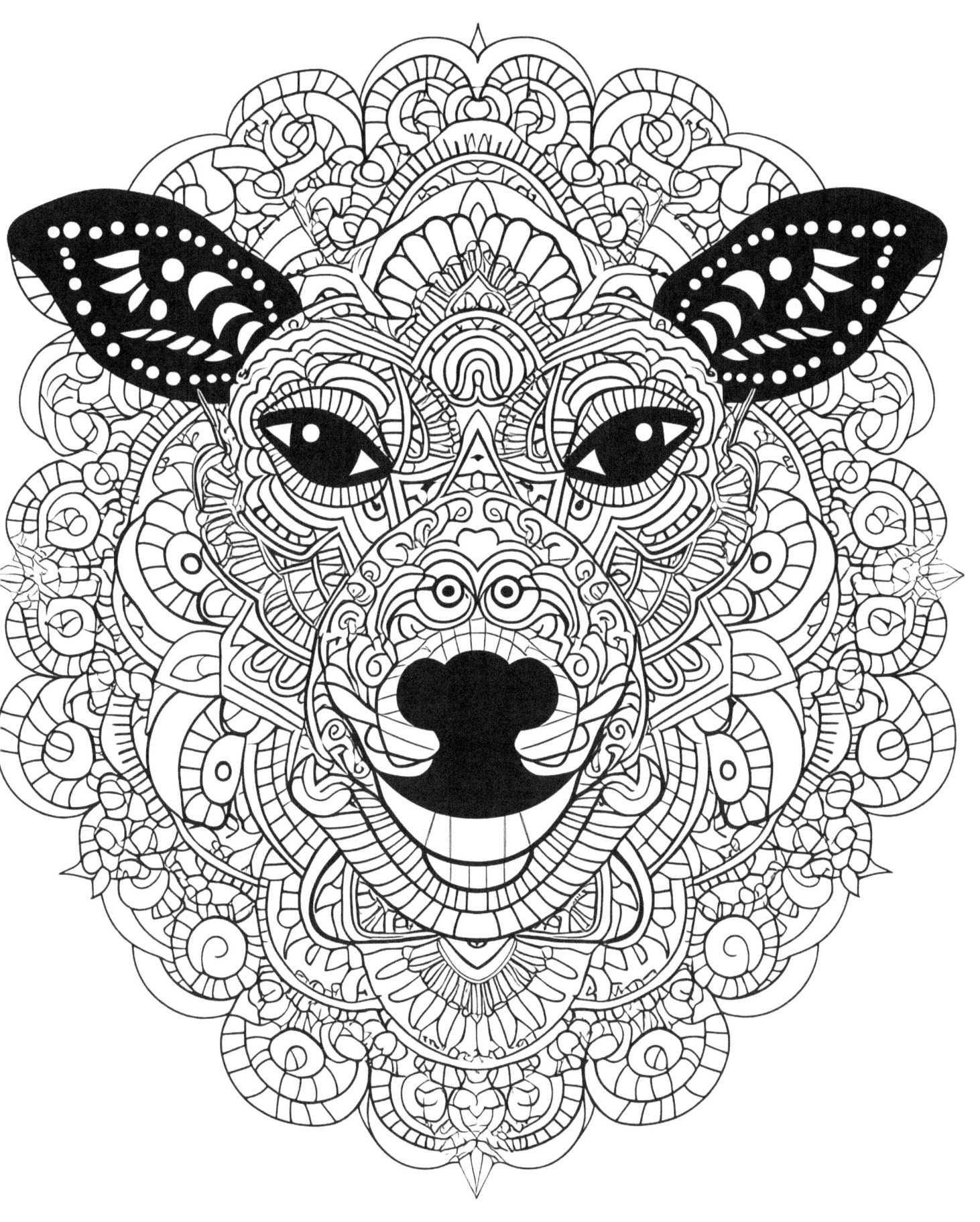

The Big Book of Mandalas & Patterns Coloring Pages
Variety Collection 1

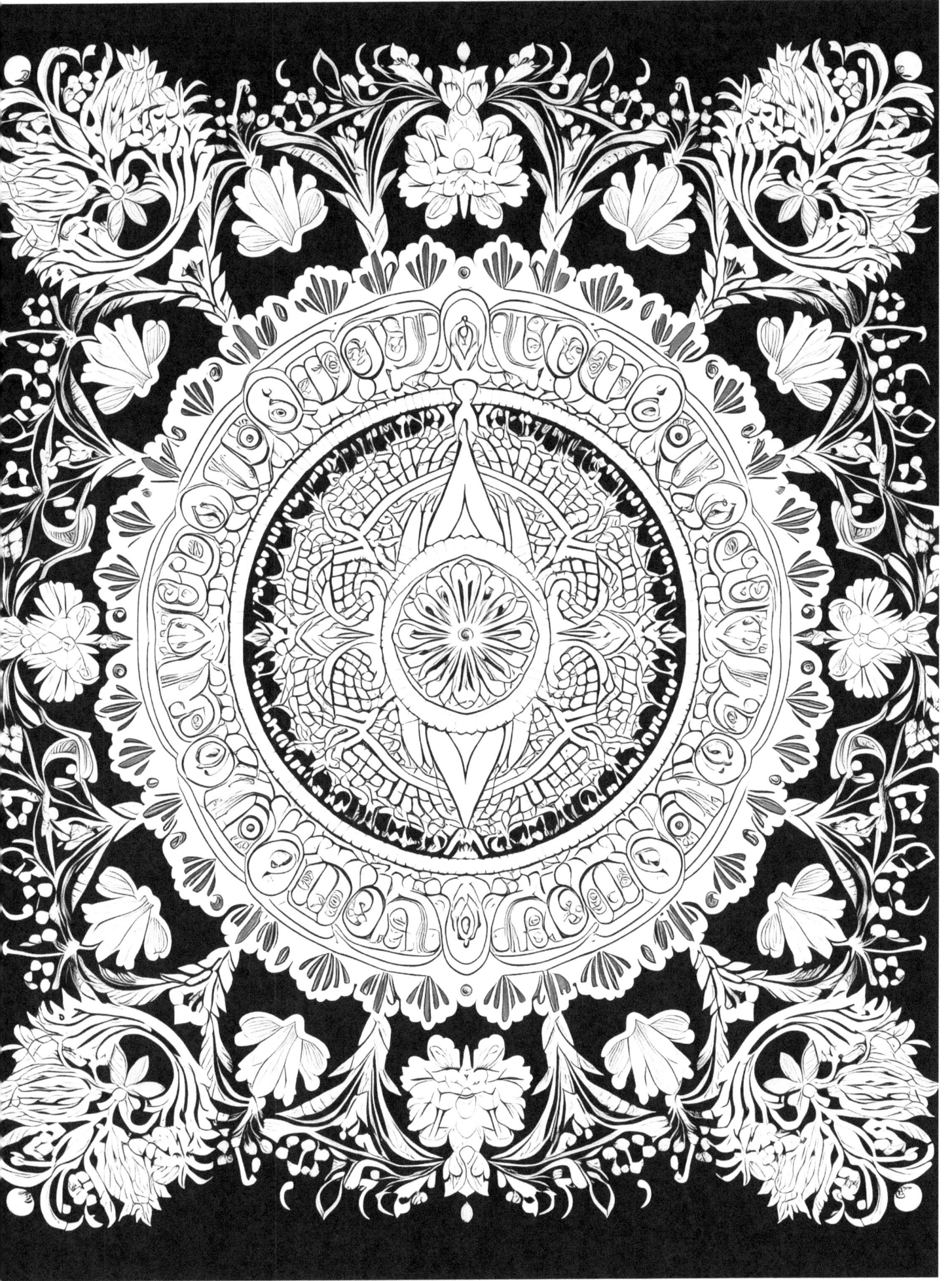

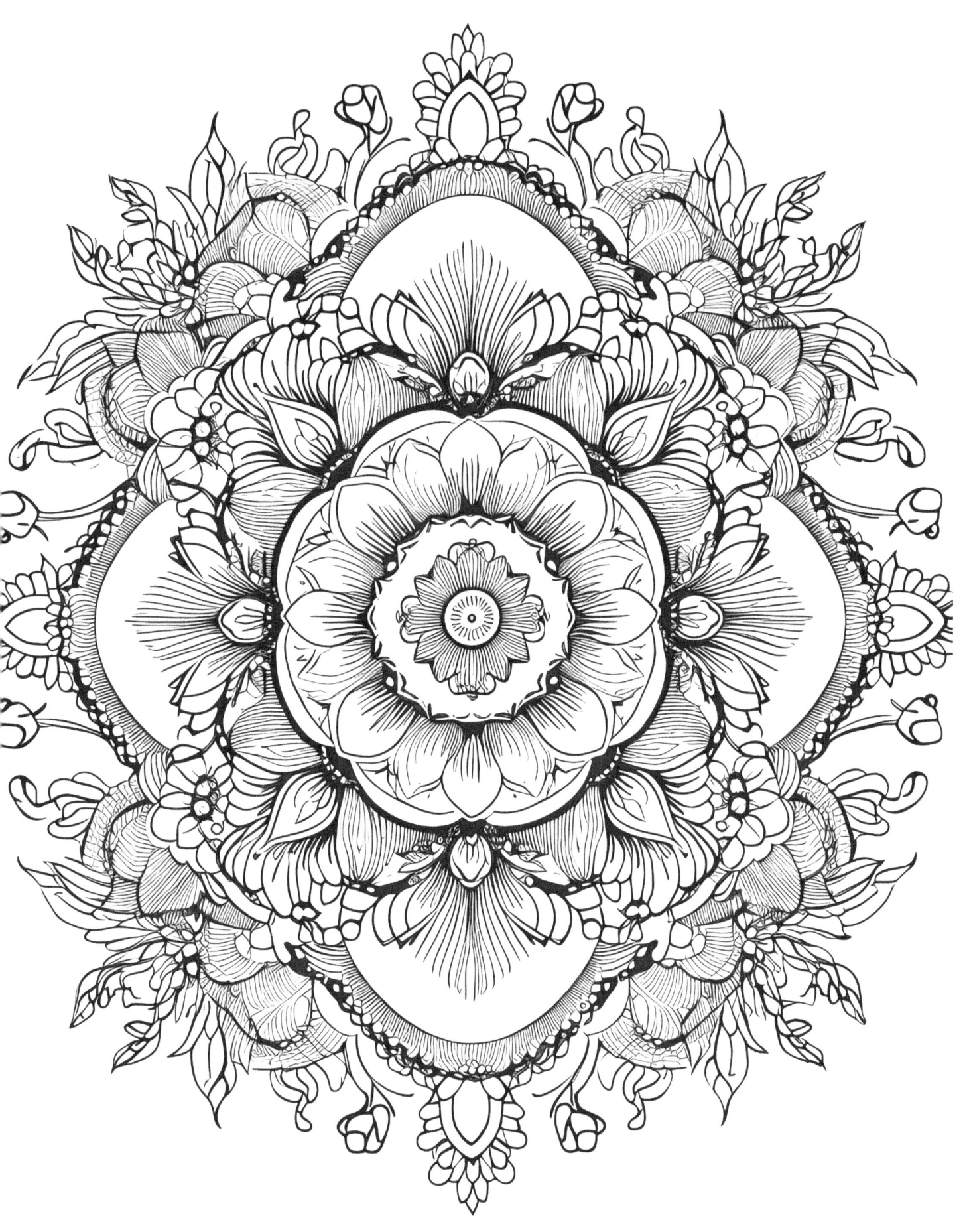

The Big Book of Mandalas & Patterns Coloring Pages
Variety Collection 1

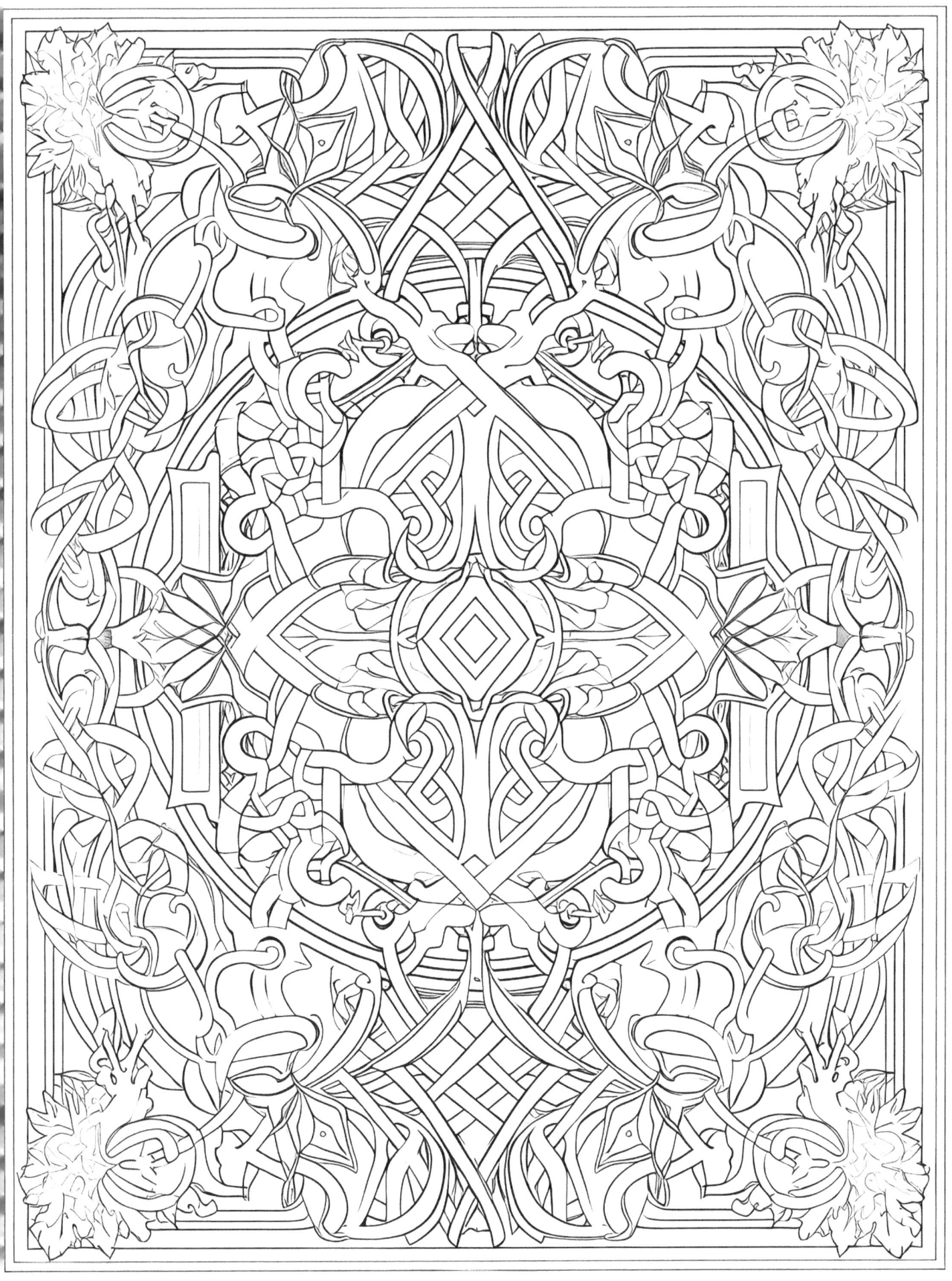

The Big Book of Mandalas & Patterns Coloring Pages
Variety Collection 1

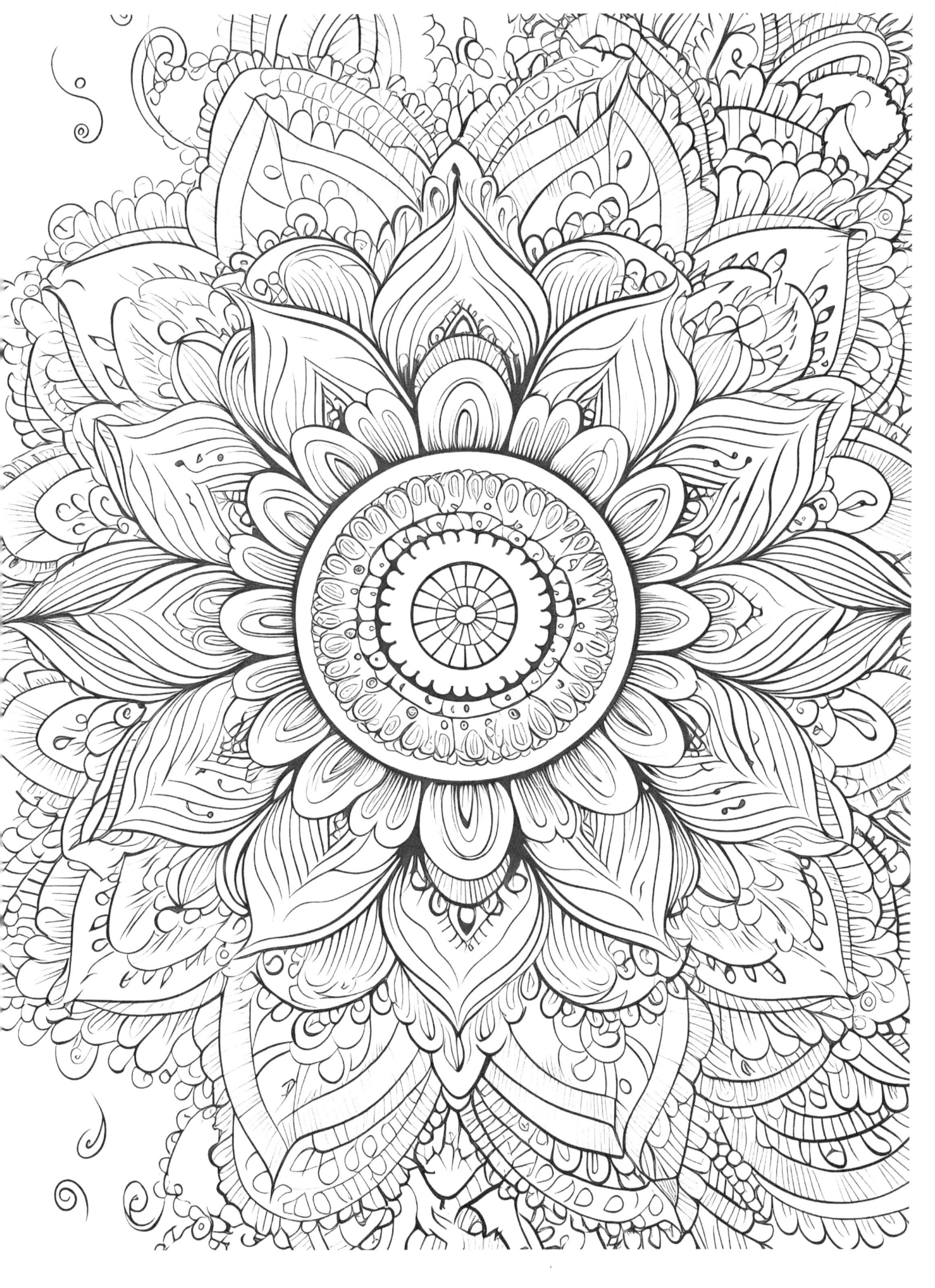

The Big Book of Mandalas & Patterns Coloring Pages
Variety Collection 1

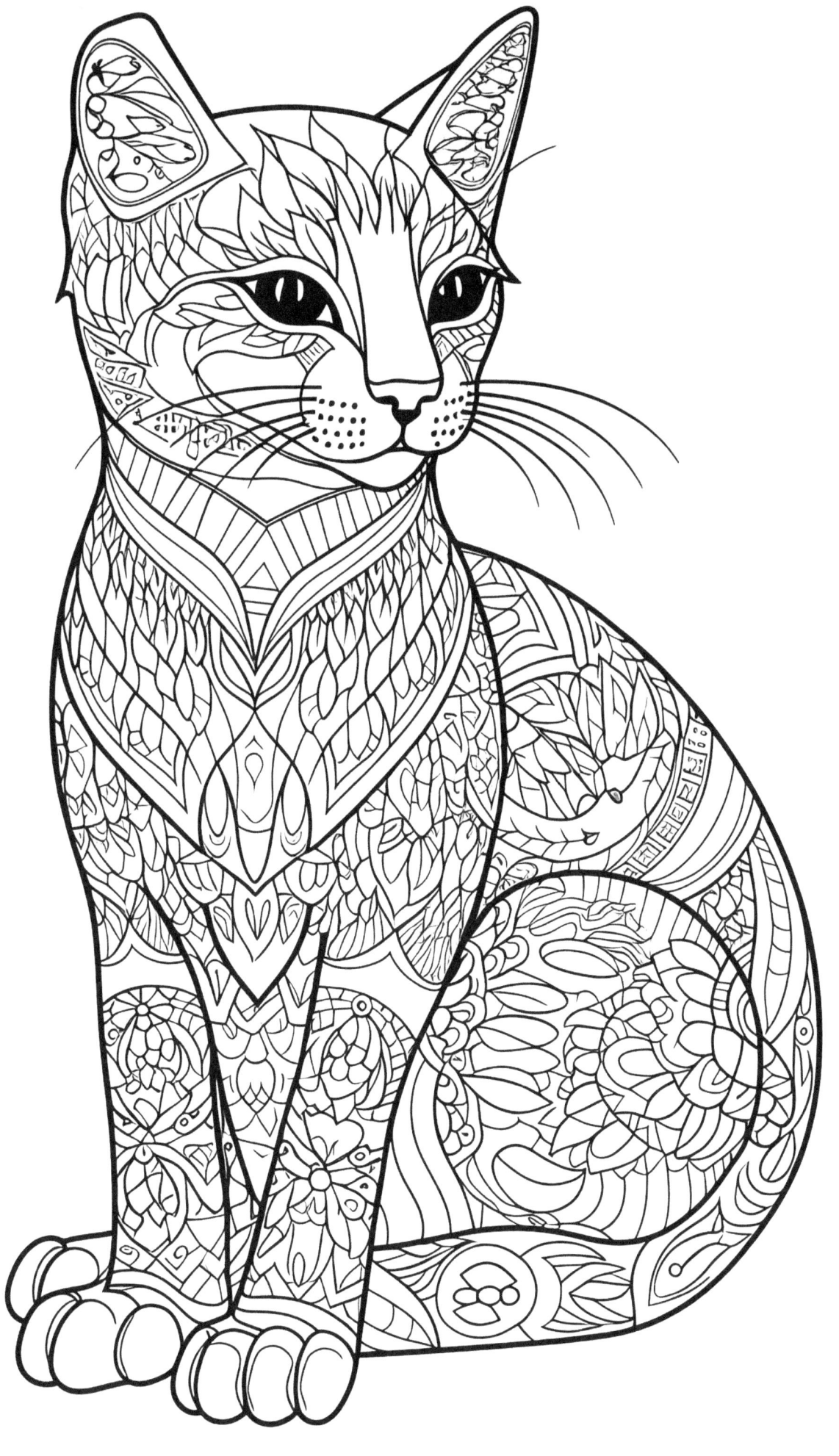

The Big Book of Mandalas & Patterns Coloring Pages
Variety Collection 1

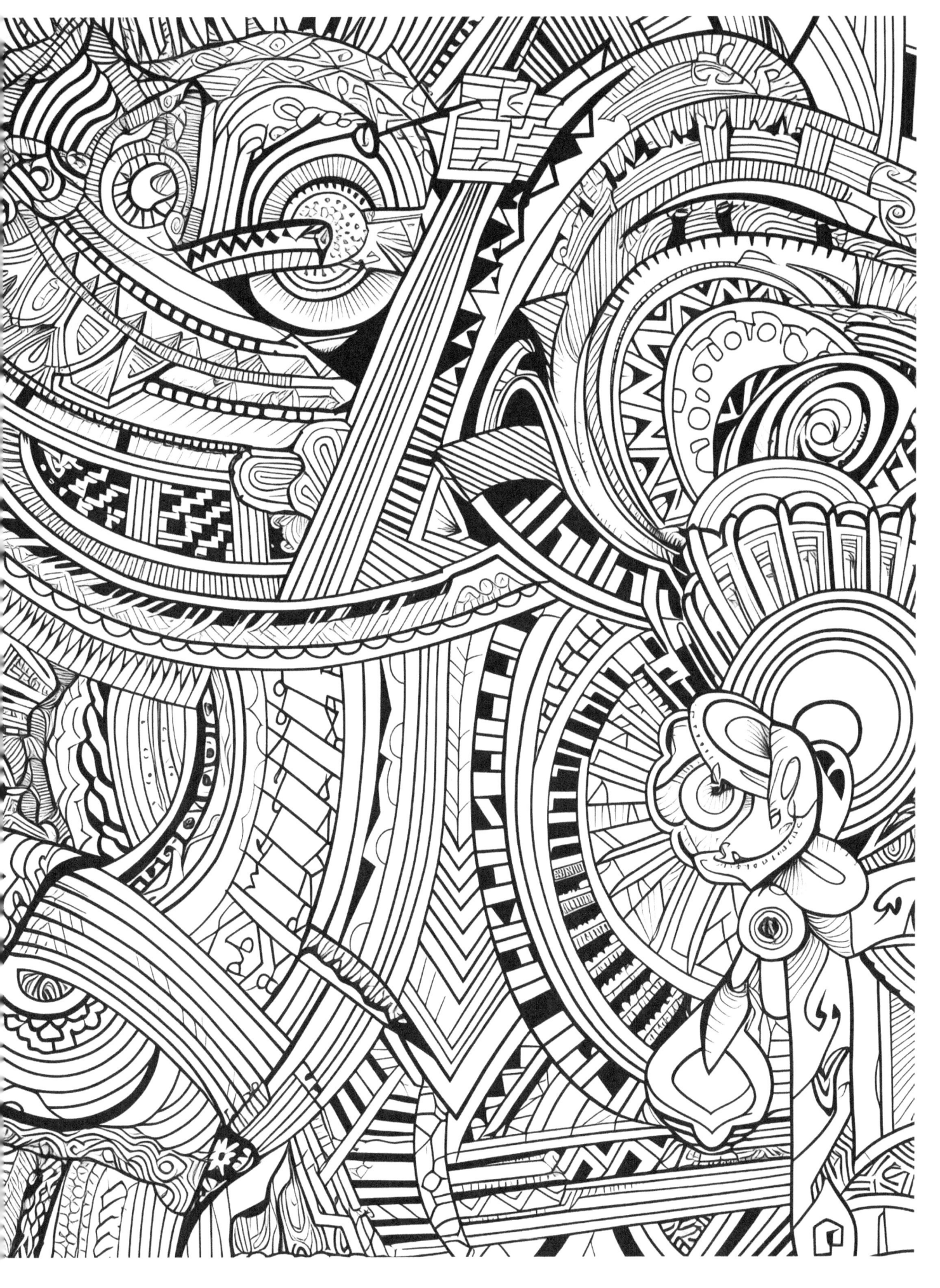

The Big Book of Mandalas & Patterns Coloring Pages
Variety Collection 1

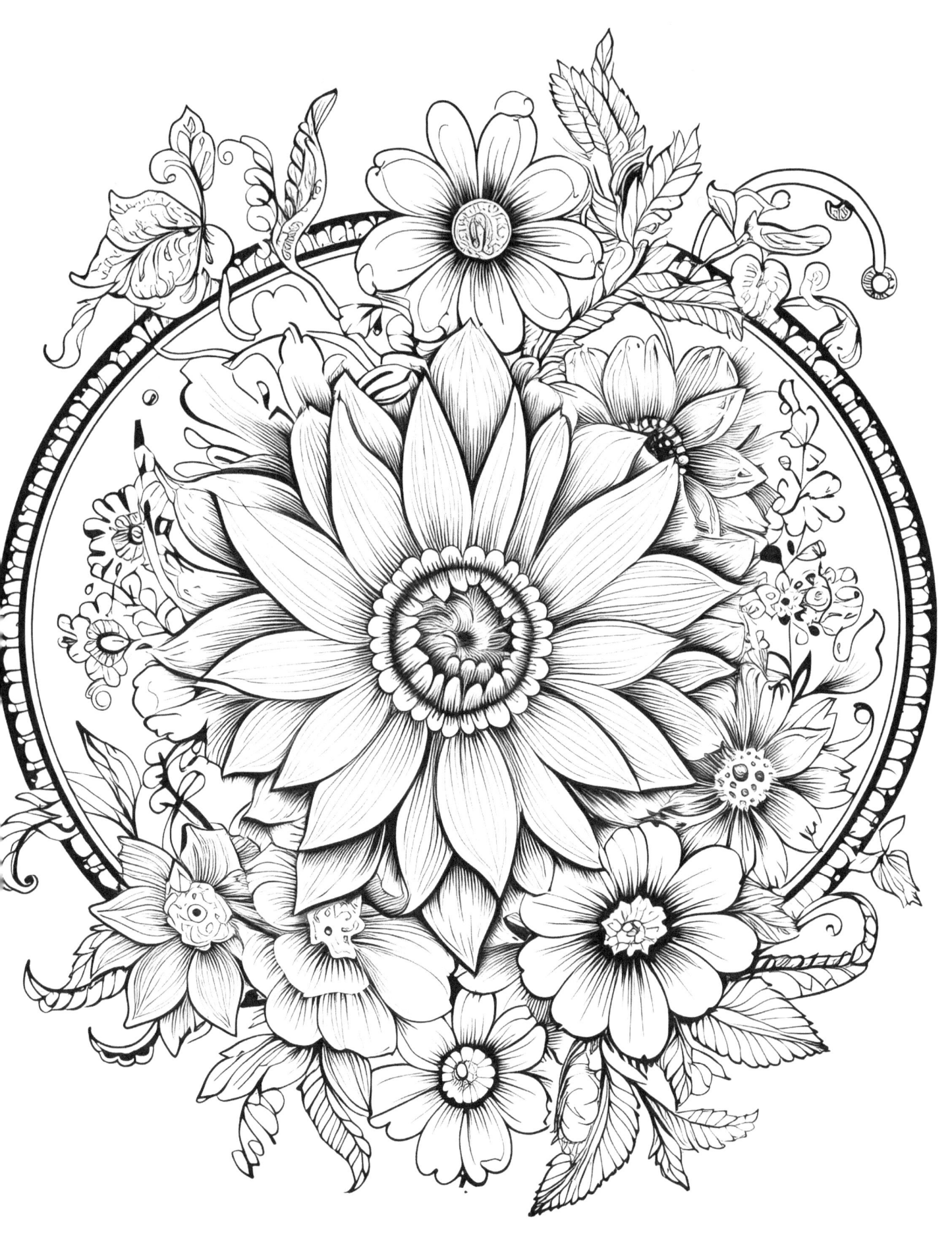

The Big Book of Mandalas & Patterns Coloring Pages
Variety Collection 1

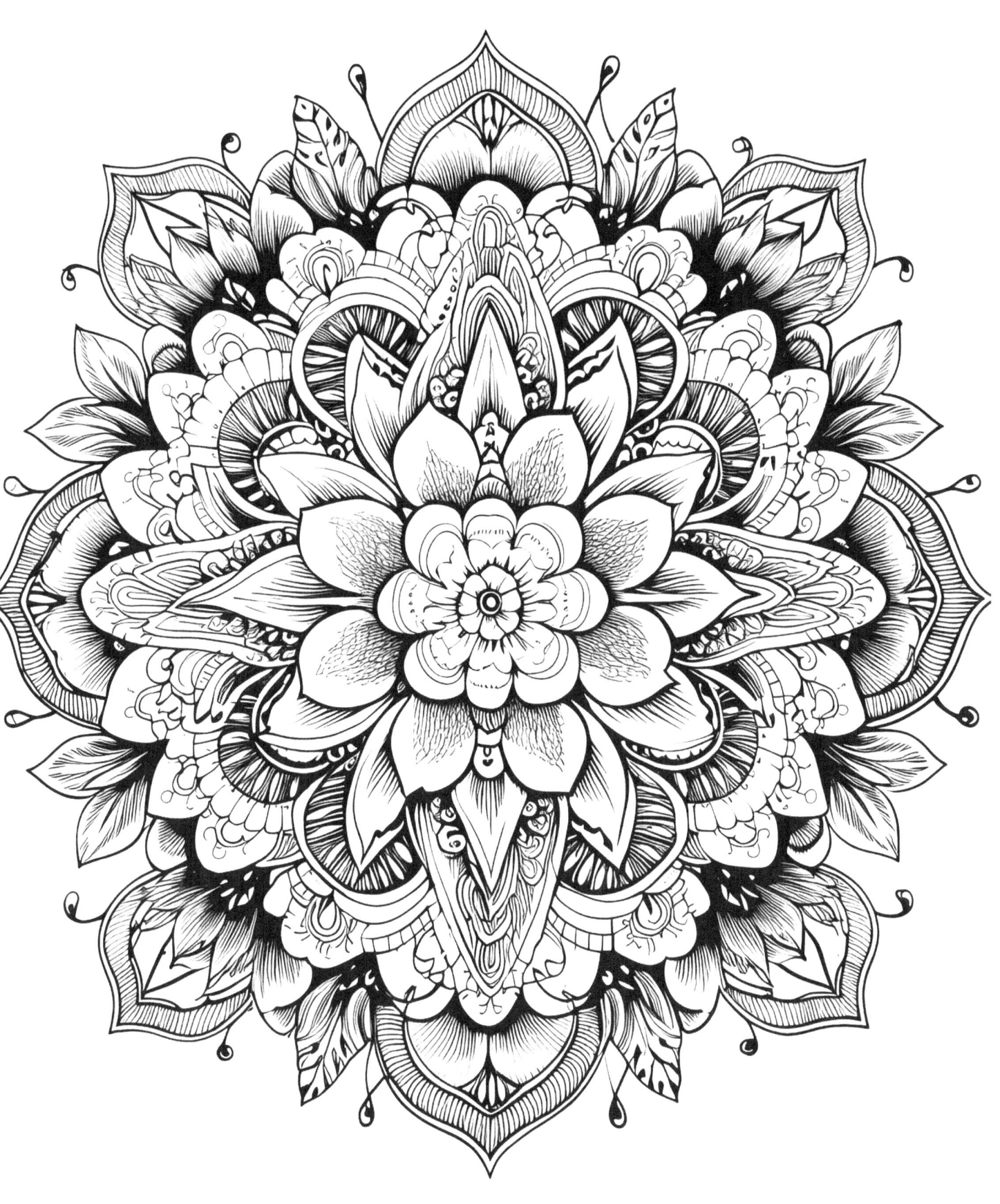

The Big Book of Mandalas & Patterns Coloring Pages
Variety Collection 1